LIZARDS
OF THE
WORLD

Chris Mattison

Facts On File
New York • Oxford

Facts on File, Inc.
460 Park Avenue South
New York, New York 10016

Library of Congress Cataloging-in-Publication Data

Mattison, Christopher.
    Lizards of the world / Chris Mattison.
       p.   cm.
    Bibliography: p.
    Includes index.
    Summary: An introduction to the origins, physical characteristics, habits, and natural environment of various species of lizards.
    ISBN 0–8160–1900–2
    1. Lizards––Juvenile literature. [1. Lizards.] I. Title.
QL666.L2M37   1989
597.95––dc19   89–1237
                                                         CIP
                                                         AC

Facts on File books are available at special discounts when purchased in bulk quantities for businesses, associations, institutions, or sales promotion. Please contact the Special Sales Department of our New York office at 212/683-2244 (dial 800-322-8755, except in NY, AK, or HI)

Composition by Ryburn Typesetting Ltd, Halifax, England.
Printed in Yugoslavia by Papirographica.

10 9 8 7 6 5 4 3 2 1

This book is printed on acid-free paper

Contents

Acknowledgements

I feel very fortunate that over the years in which I have pursued not only information on lizards, but also the lizards themselves, I have come into contact with a huge number of people who share my interest and concern for these beautiful animals. Each member of this small army has added fuel to my enthusiasm as well as allowing me to accumulate the hard facts which make a book of this type possible. No doubt many of them will recognise their comments, contributions and suggestions in the following pages. The assistance of all these people is most gratefully acknowledged, even though their names may not appear.

Several other people have accompanied me on field trips to various parts of the world and, without exception, have been unselfish in helping me to find, capture and photograph specimens, whilst others have given me free access to the animals in their collections for photographic purposes. These include the following: Bob Applegate, California Zoological Supply, Dallas Zoo, Bob Mailloux, Bill Montgomery, Mike Nolan, Jeff Nunan, John Pickett, San Diego Zoo, Terry Thatcher, Twycross Zoo, Phillipe de Vosjoli and Xotic Pets.

Special thanks go to Lee Grismer and Stephen Peltz for permission to use photographs, as indicated. Finally, thanks to the editors at Cassell for their continued support.

Introduction

There are very few parts of the world where lizards are not the most conspicuous elements of the reptile fauna. With the increasingly common migration of people to warm and sunny places for annual vacations, even those readers from the cooler latitudes will be familiar with lizards of some sort or another – for example, visitors from northern Europe to the Mediterranean region will have seen small 'wall' lizards sporting themselves on dry stone walls, alongside paths and roadsides or skittering irreverently among the tumbled ruins of earlier civilisations. In more tropical locations such as the West Indian islands, brown and green *Anolis* lizards will be seen to sun themselves on every natural, and unnatural, perch. Even more closely linked with human habits and habitations are the tropical and sub-tropical geckos, running up and down the walls of even the very best hotels and restaurants, busily gobbling up their own gourmet meals, which consist mostly of cockroaches and flies.

As a group of animals, lizards are notable, and noticeable, for their bright colours, quick movements and almost cheeky tolerance of human presence (up to a point). Because of these qualities, they rarely provoke the same kind of response as, say, snakes or toads. We can afford to look on them kindly – they amuse us and do not stir up any primeval fears or superstitions. But how much do we know about their daily lives, the things which they need in order to survive or the things which threaten their existence? Compared to many other groups of animals, we know very little, but the scientific study of lizards is gaining impetus as it becomes easier through the innovations of technology and the developments of modern methods of collecting and analysing data. Unfortunately, much of this data is presented in a form which is all but unintelligible to the average naturalist, perhaps on the assumption that he or she is not interested in, or capable of, absorbing 'scientific' information. This book is written in the belief that many 'casual' naturalists are eager to ask relevant questions about their fellow creatures, and to seek the answers, provided that these are given in a form which assumes little or no background in formal biological education, or a knowledge of the language, or jargon, of professional scientists.

There are two fundamental ways of approaching the study of biology. It is possible to look at a group of animals – insects, fishes, tapeworms, etc. – and learn everything possible about its members. This could be called the 'pigeon-hole' approach. The other method is to look at 'systems' – evolution, feeding, reproduction, etc. – themes which cut right across the natural classification and are applicable to all animals. The approach taken here is to attempt to do a little of each. The first

Plate 1. Zuni Indian fetish, depicting a horned lizard, *Phrynosoma*, carved in agate, with turquoise eyes. Lizards of this genus have long been favourite subjects in Indian art, and stylised representations can often be found in weaving and on pottery.

seven chapters deal with systems and how these systems apply to lizards (although it has sometimes been necessary to paint with a broader brush in order to fill in some fundamental principles which are necessary to an understanding of the points which have been made).

The penultimate chapter, by far the longest, caters to the pigeon-hole approach – the lizards are dealt with family by family in order to cross-reference the information given earlier. This chapter must, by necessity, be superficial; it is not possible to deal with every species in every family, or even every genus. Some animals are more interesting than others, some illustrate certain important aspects of biology, some are better known than others. The object of the exercise is not to catalogue all the known facts but to focus on those which should whet the reader's appetite for some of the more detailed and learned books and articles which are listed in the bibliography.

The final chapter deals with a group of reptiles, the amphisbaenians, which, strictly speaking, do not belong in this book, since they are not lizards. They are included only because they are a small and rather obscure group which would otherwise slip through the net of this series.

It is safe to say that we will never know all that there is to be known about lizards (or any other group of animals): parts of their lives, and the motivations for many of the things that they do will always be mysteries about which we can only speculate. The information in the following pages is a summary of the state of our knowledge up to the present time, with emphasis on the aspects of lizard biology which I hope will most appeal to the naturalist – their variety of form and colour, what makes them tick and how they interact with, and adapt to, their environment.

Finally, the reader should be aware that this interest in lizards is not new. Lizards have been the subject of speculation and superstition among our ancestors for thousands of years, especially in those areas of the world where they are most numerous. People's curiosity about the animals with which they share the earth is one of the few characteristics which sets the human being apart from other species, which are, by and large, only interested in the animals they can eat, be eaten by, or mate with. Although some of the larger lizards may play a part in the nutrition of certain groups of humans, and a very small number may cause people pain or discomfort, they normally live in peaceful coexistence with us, except when we destroy the habitat in which they live.

The current obsessions of naturalists are with research into the biology of organisms, and with saving our remaining wildlife before it disappears entirely: in the past various groups of animals, including lizards, were central to the cultures and religious beliefs of a variety of races including Australian Aborigines, North American Indians and the animists of South-East Asia. So, although the emphasis has shifted, the 'study' of lizards has always been part of human activity, and by taking an interest in their lives, the present-day naturalist is continuing a tradition which has probably been in existence as long as humans themselves.

Chapter 1
Lizards:
What They Are and Where
They Came From

It is tempting to think of lizards as little dinosaurs; leftovers from the time when their gigantic relatives were the ruling class, but, unfortunately, evolution is rarely so straightforward and it is necessary to look back into the distant past in order to give a more realistic account of their presence in the modern world.

Just as in other types of genealogy, it is always simpler to work backwards from present known relatives. In tracing the ancestry of the lizards, this can be done most simply by working back through the ages and identifying the points in time where their evolution was shaped.

Lizards are members of the order of reptiles known as the Squamata. They form the sub-order Sauria (sometimes known as Lacertilia); the other two sub-orders are the snakes (Ophidia) and the amphisbaenians (Amphisbaenia). The order first appeared about 180 million years ago during the Triassic period, arising from an extinct order known as the Eosuchia. The other surviving order from this 'stem' is the Rhynchocephalia, represented today by one solitary species, the tuatara. The Eosuchia was, in turn, part of the sub-class of reptiles known as the Lepidosaura, one of about 17 orders of reptiles which roamed the world at that time. Unfortunately for them, all but four had disappeared by the end of the Cretaceous period, about 70 million years ago, many of them perishing during the great mass extinction which devastated the animal kingdom at that time, for reasons which are still hotly debated by palaeontologists. Prior to this the reptiles had begun their heyday during the Triassic period, 230–180 million years ago, and continued to diversify and specialise to fill a variety of niches right up until the time when they were so spectacularly snuffed out. Around this same time, the earliest known fossil, showing many of the characteristics of modern lizards, *Prolacerta*, appeared.

To go back one more step, the ancestral lineage of both the reptiles and the amphibians arose during the Carboniferous period, about 300-350 million years ago. Although the amphibians continued to evolve successfully (and still do), the reptiles were able to move away from the fringes of lakes and swamps to which the amphibians were tied because of their breeding requirements, and to colonise the land completely.

The first step in this important and monumental process was the evolution of internal fertilisation. Almost all frogs and toads, and some salamanders, lay unfertilised eggs which are later exposed to the male's sperm. In an aquatic environment this system works well, but it precludes the development of a shell around the eggs, and amphibian eggs are protected only by a gelatinous coating. In order to produce an egg which is resistant to drying out, a shell must be provided, and so the sperm must be able to reach and fertilise the egg *before* the shell surrounds it – hence internal fertilisation. In addition to the shell produced by the mother, the embryo produces a second protective membrane around itself, known as the amnion.

A further complication involves the development of the embryo. The normal amphibian life cycle includes a free-living aquatic larval stage (tadpole), which is capable of feeding and providing itself with the additional material necessary for its subsequent growth and metamorphosis. A shelled egg, on the other hand, must contain all the materials needed by the embryonic animal to see it through its development. This necessitates the provision of a large yolk to nourish the embryo. The technical term to describe eggs with large yolks is telolecithal, and the reptiles were the first animals to produce a telolecithal, amniotic egg.

The evolution of a scaly integument which, although not totally impervious to water, did allow them to withstand conditions which were considerably drier than those to which the amphibians are restricted, completed the equipment which enabled the reptiles to undertake the colonisation of the land.

It has been postulated that many of the early reptiles were herbivorous, feeding on plants which were, at that time, also in a state of evolutionary flux. It is thought that the development of toxic tannins by those plants may have been one of the causes of the decline of several groups of reptiles, notably the dinosaurs. (Not all dinosaurs were herbivorous, of course, but those which were not will have relied heavily on their vegetarian relatives to provide them with meat.) Another theory which has been mooted to account for the decline of the large reptiles is one of changing climatic conditions. Since all reptiles are ectotherms, relying on outside sources for their energy, any small drop in radiant heat would have had disastrous results, especially on the larger forms which would (a) take longer to warm up, and (b) have such long generation times that their ability to adapt would have been considerably reduced compared with that of the smaller species, which have shorter generation times. The surviving large reptiles, such as the crocodiles and large turtles, are all restricted to tropical or sub-tropical parts of the world. (This is not the full story, however, since many other groups of animals, for instance the ammonites, disappeared at about the same time. As they neither ate land plants nor were subject to temperature variations, other events occurring around the same time, possibly meteorite damage or the movement of the continental plates, must also be taken into the reckoning.)

Whatever the reason for the elimination of the majority of reptiles, and the most spectacular ones at that, the few surviving groups, including the squamates, no doubt benefited from the sudden lack of competition (competitive release), although they may have had this advantage undermined by the emergence of another group of animals which had been waiting on the sidelines for some time, perfectly placed to exploit the niches vacated by the dinosaurs. These, of course, were the mammals.

What remains, therefore, is a series of survivors, or at least the descendants of survivors, which, in the case of the Squamata, now contains about 6,000 species in all, about half of which are lizards, 130 amphisbaenians and the rest snakes. The other three surviving orders of reptiles, which have been nowhere near as successful in diversifying, are the Chelonia (turtles) with about 225 species, the Crocodilia (crocodiles and alligators) with 21 species, and the lonely tuatara with no living close relatives.

What makes a lizard different from (a) the other squamates, and (b) other reptiles which are superficially similar to it, i.e. the crocodilians and the tuatara? First, lizards differ from snakes and amphisbaenians in possessing four legs and movable eyelids. Those species which have lost their legs due to a burrowing life-style still retain the limb girdles to which the legs would have been attached had they been present. Even the most primitive snakes possess only the hind (pelvic) limb girdle. Similarly, the amphisbaenians have also lost their legs (with the

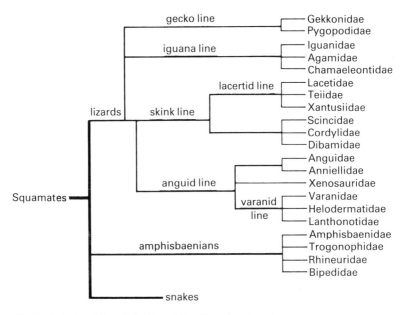

Fig. 1. Relationships of the lizard families, showing the four major ancestral lines, while the list opposite gives details of the number of species in each family.

The families of lizards

Family (popular name)	approx. no. of species
Gekkotans (gecko line)	
Gekkonidae (geckos) **	830
Pygopodidae (flap-footed lizards) **	31
Iguanians (iguana line)	
Iguanidae (iguanids)	650
Agamidae (agamids)	300
Chamaeleontidae (chameleons)	85
Scincomorphs (skink line)	
Lacertidae (lacertids)	200
Teiidae (whiptails)	227
Xantusiidae (night lizards)	16
Scincidae (skinks)	1000+
Cordylidae (girdle-tailed and plated lizards)	50
Dibamidae	10
Anguinomorphs (anguid line)	
Anguidae (legless lizards and alligator lizards)	75
Anniellidae *	2
Xenosauridae (crocodile lizards)	4
Varanidae (monitors)	30
Helodermatidae (Gila monster and beaded lizard)	2
Lanthanotidae (earless monitor)	1
Total	3513+

* **Note:** the anniellids are sometimes combined with the Anguidae.
** **Note:** see page 105 for recent proposals concerning the reclassification of the gekkotans.

exception of one genus, *Bipes*, in which the forelegs have been retained), but amphisbaenians are anatomically different in other ways, such as the annular arrangement of their scales. Lizards are distinct from the crocodilians and the tuatara, to which they bear a superficial resemblence, due to the arrangement of their scales and the fundamental differences in the shape of their skull, a characteristic which forms the basis of the classification of reptiles due to its adaptive significance.

The surviving lizard species are grouped into units containing species which are closely related to each other. It is generally agreed that there were four 'ancestral lines' of lizards, which were separated from one another millions of years ago. The families which developed from these lines share certain basic characteristics and are sometimes grouped together as 'infra-orders'. The four lines consist of the gekkotans, the iguanians, the scincomorphs and the anguinomorphs.

A simple definition of a species is 'a population of animals which can reproduce under natural conditions to form fertile offspring'. Although this definition is not totally watertight – hybrids do occur occasionally and, under artificial conditions, can also often be created – the species is the universally accepted way of distinguishing between distinct populations of animals. Species which, although distinct, are obviously closely related and are derived from a common ancestry in the not too distant past are grouped together into genera (singular genus). The genus forms the first part of the scientific name of each species, written in italics and given a capital letter, e.g. *Lacerta*, and the species forms the second name, e.g. *viridis*, also written in italics, but without a capital letter (even if it is derived from a proper name, e.g. *madagascariensis*). Genera which have close affinities with each other are, in turn, grouped together into families, and these families form a convenient way of dividing a large group of species into fairly manageable units, although they are not all of equal size.

Most authorities recognise 16 or 17 families of lizards and these are listed in the table on page 13, with the approximate number of species in each. Unfortunately, many families of lizards (and very many species) have not acquired universally accepted English common names and so it is necessary to refer to them constantly by their Latinised labels. This may appear intimidating to many naturalists, especially if they are used to dealing with groups such as birds in which common names are used almost exclusively, but there is little point in inventing common names for those lizards which do not have them. For this reason it has been necessary to use Latinised names in the following chapters. It is worth pointing out, however, that if at any stage during the following pages the reader becomes bogged down in words which are difficult to spell and even more difficult to pronounce, he or she should disregard them – it is not essential to become *au fait* with the nomenclature in order to understand the principles discussed, and knowing the Latin name of a species is not nearly so important as understanding what makes it tick.

14

Chapter 2
Form and Function

Lizards exist in a variety of shapes, sizes and colours. They range in size from tiny, delicate and secretive creatures to huge, dragon-like marauders; they may have four legs, two legs or no legs at all, and are frequently adorned with embellishments such as crests, horns, flaps and frills. There is a serious purpose behind each of these characteristics, as well as behind the variation itself, and each has evolved because in some way it increases that species' chance of survival. Superimposed on this is the natural tendency for closely related species to share certain characteristics because they originate from common ancestors. The size and shape of each lizard is therefore due to a combination of two factors: adaptation to its environment and its evolutionary history.

Plate 2. *Phrynosoma modestum*, the round-tailed horned lizard, a good example of a short, stout lizard. Species such as this rely on camouflage rather than speed and agility for protection, and prey on insects which are easily captured.

SIZE

Lengths of lizards are sometimes given as total lengths (TL), i.e. from the snout to the tip of the tail, or as snout–vent lengths (SVL), which is especially useful in the case of those species in which individuals lose their tail. Most species fall within the range 15–60 cm (6–24 in) total length, but there is a great deal of variation. The smallest species are among the geckos, particularly the South American members of the family. Several members of the genus *Sphaerodactylus*, for instance, are full grown at less than 10 cm (4 in), while some measure less than 6 cm (2 in), of which about half is tail. Other small species include several of the night lizards, microteiids and skinks.

The largest species of lizard is almost certainly the Komodo dragon, *Varanus komodoensis*, which may measure 3 m (10 ft) in total length and weigh over 150 kg (330 lb). This species is known to have killed and eaten humans, although its normal diet consists largely of carrion. Other *Varanus* species approach this size, for instance the New Guinea monitor, *V. salvadorii*, which can be as long, perhaps even longer, than the Komodo dragon although far less bulky, the Australian perentie, *V. giganteus*, which may grow to 2.5 m (7.5 ft), the lace monitor, *V. varius*, also from Australia, which grows to 2 m (5 ft), and the African Nile monitor, *Varanus niloticus*, also at about 2 metres. All of these are impressive animals which defend themselves fiercely if cornered.

The largest South American species is the common iguana, *Iguana iguana*, which approaches 2 m (5 ft) in total length; in North America two species of glass lizards grow to about 100 cm (39 in) while the Gila monster, *Heloderma suspectum*, a much bulkier animal, grows to 50 cm (19.5 in). In Europe the legless species *Ophisaurus apodus* grows to a total length of 120 cm (47 in), although two-thirds of this is tail. The largest amphisbaenian is *Amphisbaena alba*, from South America, which grows to about 75 cm (29.5 in).

SHAPE

Like humans, lizards can be short and stout or long and thin, with all sorts of variations in between. The extremes are probably represented on the one hand by the horned lizards, *Phrynosoma* spp., from North America, which are saucer-shaped with a large head and a short tail, and on the other by the Australian legless snake lizards such as *Lialis burtoni*, which grows to 50 cm (19.5 in) or more, although it is no thicker than a pencil at mid-body, and numerous other legless lizards or species with reduced legs (Plates 3 and 4).

General body outline is associated to a large extent with the life-style and method of locomotion of the lizard: slender, sinuous species tend to be those which move rapidly through dense vegetation or through sand or soil; heavily built species are slow-moving and often feed on vegetation or easily captured prey. Species which are forced to undergo long periods of time with little or no food also tend to be more heavily built – their extra bulk provides the space for stored fat.

Plate 3. *Lialis burtoni* represents the opposite extreme from Plate 2 – a slender elongated species without legs, which relies more on speed to escape predators and capture its prey.

Apart from the overall body shape, the size and shape of the legs and tail are often good indicators of a lizard's life-style, and these show a number of interesting adaptations to different modes of life.

THE LEGS

Typical lizards have four well-developed legs, the hind ones usually being longer and more powerful than the front ones. Lizard locomotion takes the form of moving one front leg and the opposite hind leg forward at the same time. The legs then alternate and the animal wriggles forward (Fig. 2). In some species, the hind legs have become disproportionately muscular and these are used as the main locomotive force. When moving rapidly, these species sometimes lift their front legs off the ground completely and run only on their hind legs (Fig. 3). This is known as bipedal locomotion and is especially common among iguanids, agamids and monitor lizards. The basilisk lizard of South America, an iguanid, has extended this technique to include running rapidly across the surface of water, and is locally known as the 'Jesus Christ' lizard. The technique has also been taken to extremes in several monitor lizards, and in the frilled lizard, *Chlamydosaurus kingii*, all of which raise the front of their bodies from the ground at the slightest provocation and may even stand on their hind legs to survey their surroundings or to confront their aggressors.

A completely opposite strategy is to reduce the size of the legs, or to dispense with them altogether. This invariably occurs together with elongation of the body. Members of several families have reduced or absent legs.

Pygopodidae The front legs are absent, and the hind limbs are reduced to barely noticeable scaly flaps in all species.

Teiidae A few species have reduced legs, e.g. *Bachia cophias* and *B. trinasale* from South America, which have tiny front limbs and hind limbs which are reduced to stumps.

Scincidae The tendency towards reduction of the limbs is very strong in this family and there are many species without limbs, e.g. *Ophiomorus punctatissimus* from eastern Europe and *Acontias* spp. from southern Africa, even more with very small legs, e.g. *Chalcides chalcides*, the seps, and some with only a pair of back legs, e.g. *Lerista bipes*, *L. labialis*, etc. from Australia. Some genera show a complete gradation from legs to 'leglessness', e.g. *Chalcides*.

Cordylidae Reduction of the limbs is found only in the members of the genus *Chamaesaurus* from southern Africa, such as *C. macrolepis*, in which the front limbs are absent altogether and the hind limbs are small spikes – in the other species all four limbs are present but very reduced.

Dibamidae All members of this small family are virtually limbless, although males have short stump-like hind legs.

Anguidae As with the skinks, a whole range of limb conditions is found in this family. In several *Diploglossus*, from the West Indies, the limbs are small, and in *Ophisaurus* from Europe, Asia and North America, they are completely absent.

Anniellidae Both members of this small family are completely legless.

Plate 4. *Ophisaurus ventralis* is one member of the anguidae in which the legs are absent. Legless lizards are also found in several other families.

Fig. 2. Locomotion in a typical lizard. The lizard moves its diagonally opposite front and hind legs forward together, causing the body to wriggle as it progresses.

Fig. 3. Bipedal locomotion. At speed the front feet are raised off the ground and the lizard uses only its powerful hind limbs.

A number of the plates (e.g. 4, 5, and 96) show lizards which have reduced or absent legs. The gradual loss of limbs in these unrelated lizards therefore represents a striking example of convergent evolution. In most instances, the reduction of legs probably began as an adaptation to burrowing, but not all species live beneath the ground. Some live among thick vegetation where long limbs would be a hindrance, and some legless lizards, such as the glass lizards, *Ophiosaurus* (Plate 4) also climb up into low bushes as well as living among grass and ground-covering plants. Species with small legs may use them when crawling slowly, but lie them flat alongside their body and resort to a serpentine method of locomotion when moving rapidly or burrowing; for instance, the group of desert skinks known collectively as 'sandfish' (Plate 5).

It is interesting to note that snakes probably evolved from an early stock of lizards which lost their limbs as a result of a burrowing existence, and that the amphisbaenians are comprised solely of burrowing species, all of which are without limbs except the three strange species of *Bipes*, in which the front limbs are retained (see Chapter 10).

Apart from supplying the power of locomotion, the limbs also serve other purposes in many lizards. Burrowing species, such as the Gila monster, have powerful forelegs and long claws with which they dig, either to provide a retreat for themselves or to root out prey. A species of gecko from south-west Africa, *Palmatogecko rangei* (Plate 63), has webbed feet which help it to move over the surface of fine sand in the deserts where it lives, while another species, *Kaokogecko vanzyli*, has webbed hind feet. Geckos of the genus *Ptychozoon* (Plate 7), which are South-East Asian, also have webbed feet, but for a completely different reason. These species have a fold of skin running along each side of the body. When they launch themselves from tall trees they spread their toes and flaps, and glide down to the ground or to another tree-trunk, rather like a paper dart. These species are known, predictably, as 'flying geckos'.

THE TAIL
Tails serve a variety of purposes in a variety of lizards. Species which run on their hind legs lift their tail and use it as a counterbalance; the tails of these species are usually long. Other species use their tails when climbing, either for balance, much as a mouse uses its tail (or a tight-rope walker uses a pole), or as a fifth limb. Chameleons are the most obvious examples of lizards which use their tails for grasping (Plate 8), but other species, such as the Solomon Islands skink, *Corucia zebrata*, and the geckos belonging to the genera *Naultinus* and *Heteropholis*, which are arboreal species endemic to New Zealand, also have prehensile tails.

Other lizards use their tails to store fat reserves for use during hibernation, aestivation or periods of food shortage. In these species the tail may become enlarged and turnip-shaped, for instance in the beaded lizards, genus *Heloderma*, and in many species of desert-dwelling geckos

Plate 5. The sandfish is a species of skink, adapted for life in dunes, where it 'swims' beneath the surface of the sand.

Plate 6. The tails of *Nephrurus* geckos, from Australia, are short and bulbous, and may end in a knob. This is *N. laevis.*

such as *Eublepharis macularius* (Plate 58) from Asia and some of the *Diplodactylus* species from Australia. The latter genus also contains several species which are able to secrete a smelly mucus from glands in their tails as a means of defence, and one of these species, *Diplodactylus ciliaris*, has an additional armoury in the form of a double row of small spines running along the length of its tail (Plate 9). The tail is also used in other defence strategies, for instance blocking burrows and crevices and as a sacrificial offering, as described in Chapter 5.

Australian geckos of the genus *Phyllurus* have strange leaf-shaped tails (Plate 63 and Fig. 8), while those of *Nephrurus*, also from Australia, have tails which end in a small knob-like structure (Plate 6). The functions of neither type of tail are known for certain. In Asia, but still with the gecko family, *Ptychozoon* spp. have a scallop-shaped fringe around the edge of the tail, and this enhances these species' ability to glide (see page 21).

TOES

Geckos are best known for their ability to run on smooth vertical surfaces and even to cling upside down on ceilings, etc. (although not

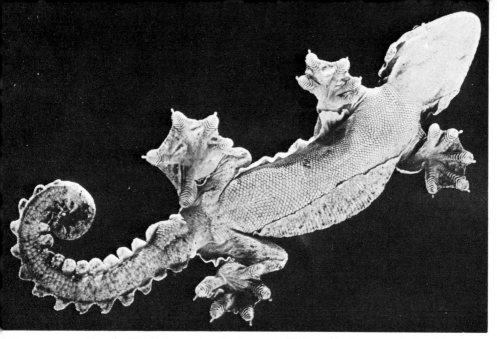

Plate 7. The flying gecko, *Ptychozoon kuhli*, has adhesive toe-pads for climbing, as well as webbed feet and a flap of skin along its flanks for gliding.

Plate 8. The prehensile tail of a chameleon, which is usually coiled like a watch spring when not in use.

Plate 9. The tail of *Diplodactylus ciliaris* has a double row of short spines along its length. It also contains glands which fire a noxious sticky substance when the lizard is alarmed.

Plate 10. Before raising its foot, a climbing gecko must curl its toes away from the surface in order to disengage the adhesive pads.

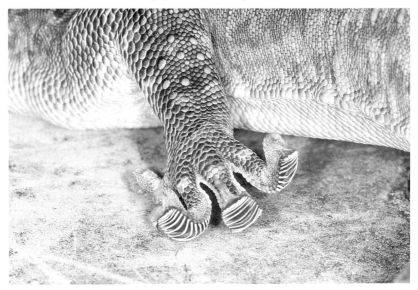

every species is so endowed). The secret of their 'stickability' is in their feet. Each digit is splayed out at the end and the pads so formed are covered with numerous microscopic bristles. Although the bristles end in disc-shaped structures, they do not act like suckers as geckos are unable to cling to smooth *wet* surfaces. It is assumed instead that each bristle finds a tiny irregularity in the surface and the gecko is able to attach itself through their cumulative efforts, rather like the individual strands of Velcro. This system works very well, but how does the gecko manage to run, or even jump, when the soles of its feet stick like glue? As Plate 10 shows, immediately before each foot is lifted the gecko's toes curl up at the ends in order to disengage the bristles. Other climbing species, such as *Anolis* lizards, also have toe-pads, although these are less well developed than those of the geckos.

The toes of several species of lizards which live among sand dunes, e.g. *Acanthodactylus* spp. from the Mediterranean region, and *Uma* spp. from the deserts of North America, have a row of elongated scales along each digit. These 'fringe-toed' species are thus able to run rapidly across loose sand.

SCALES

Lizard scales are formed from areas of thickened skin, and their shape, size and arrangement show a wide variation, from large overlapping tile-like structures to small granular nodules. Many lizards have scales of different types distributed over various parts of their bodies; for instance, those on the head may be large and symmetrically arranged, whereas those on the body are smaller. The scales of many species are thickened to form a kind of 'armour-plating' which protects the lizard from desiccation as well as from predators. Good examples of these species are the zonures, *Cordylus* spp. from Africa, and the alligator lizards, *Gerrhonotus* spp., from North America. At the other extreme, many species of geckos have fragile, tissue-like skin covered with minute granular scales, often creating a velvety appearance. The scales of the stump-tailed skink (Plate 13) are among the largest, consisting of very thick, irregularly shaped plates, so that the lizard has a texture similar to a fir-cone. *Heloderma* scales (Plate 15) consist of thick, roughly circular 'studs' arranged in regular rows, while those of chameleons are similar in structure but show much variation in size so that a single large scale may be surrounded by many smaller and intermediate ones. Skinks normally have highly polished overlapping scales (Plate 11), giving them a shiny appearance, with the exception of the stump-tailed skink, *Trachysaurus rugosus*, mentioned above, and several of the *Egernia* spp. which have large, raised scales (Plate 14). Lizards in a number of families, including the lacertids and the night lizards, have rows of large rectangular scales on their undersides. The skink, *Fojia bumui*, has a most unusual arrangement of scales: small granular scales cover the flanks and most of the back, except for a few rows of large scales arranged along the mid-dorsal line.

Ptychozoon developed in order to enhance its camouflage; when the lizard is resting on a tree-trunk they break up its outline and tend to eliminate its shadow. The flaps have no skeletal support and are opened by air resistance during gliding. In *Draco*, the wings are supported by elongated ribs and can be opened and closed voluntarily. Each species has a different pattern on its wings, and they are also used during territorial displays, much as the *Anolis* lizards use their dewlaps. In Africa a single species of lacertid, the blue-tailed tree lizard, *Holaspis guentheri*, seems to be in a transitional stage – its tail and toes are fringed by large flattened scales which may serve to reduce air resistance and enable some degree of stability when it leaps from tree to tree, which it has been observed to do on occasions. It is interesting that in South America, where there is a large number of arboreal lizards, nothing similar has evolved.

COLOUR

Colour is an important aspect of lizard biology for several reasons. Because lizards are the most visually orientated of the reptiles, patches of bright colour are important in communication between individuals. Colour is also important in helping the lizard to blend into its surroundings and thereby escape the notice of predators. These two requirements seem to be at odds with each other, and many species compromise. Thus, many lizards have brightly coloured undersides, or patches of bright colour on their flanks and throats (Plate 48). When displaying to one another, these lizards expose their bright flash markings by raising their bodies up in a series of push-ups (Fig. 12). Others signal by raising and lowering coloured flaps, as in the *Anolis* and *Draco* species already mentioned.

In the majority of species, it is only the male which is colourful, the females being much duller and well camouflaged. The reason behind this is that females may be more vulnerable when they are carrying the extra burden of a developing clutch of eggs or young, apart from the fact that it is normally the male's job to defend a territory and to attract a mate – the onus of communicating at a distance therefore lies with him, whereas all the female has to do is to respond to his signals if she so desires. Selection for bright colours can also occur even when these are detrimental – males which are brightest have the best chance of attracting mates and passing on their genes, even though this may make them more vulnerable to predation. Dull males are not so likely to be eaten but rarely become fathers. Bright courtship colours are therefore a trade-off between reproductive success and predator avoidance!

Colour may also play a part in the absorption of solar radiation, as described in Chapter 3, and so, as a rule, lizards which live at more northerly and southerly latitudes and at higher altitudes tend to be rather darker in colour than those from warm places, and activities such as display must take second place to thermal requirements.

The nature of the various colours with which lizards are adorned may

35

be chemical or physical. Pigments in the cells near the surface form the basis of chemical colouration, whereas the position of reflective or light-scattering cellular particles may provide an additional colour or colours.

COLOUR CHANGE

Many species of lizards are able to change colour over a fairly short period of time. Rapid colour change is brought about by altering the shape of the cells which contain pigment, and is controlled by hormones. Colour change may occur for a variety of reasons, temperature control being one. Dark pigments absorb heat more readily than light ones and so lizards often become darker when they are cold and paler when they are warm. This technique is often very noticeable in desert species which need to warm up quickly in the morning and then prolong their period of activity by reflecting heat when the sun becomes stronger.

In the case of chameleons, the most famous of the quick-change artists, changes of colour and pattern are more to do with the 'mood' of the animal than with the background it is resting on, and their ability to adapt to their surroundings is often highly exaggerated. When a chameleon is frightened or provoked, its pattern may change from plain green or brown to one of strongly contrasting bars, stripes or spots. Patterns also change in response to the presence of another member of the same species, whether of the same or the opposite sex, and can then be thought of as a means of communication. Similarly, the colour of males of many species may intensify when confronted with a rival, and this is usually accompanied by characteristic postures or movements. *Anolis* lizards are also adept at colour changes, and one species, *A. carolinensis*, is sometimes called the 'American chameleon'. These lizards are also stimulated to change colour by the intensity of light, temperature and social interactions, but males are often more 'changeable' than females and their repertoire usually includes the more striking colour combinations.

Finally, males of many lizards gradually change colour in preparation for the breeding season, probably as a result of increased testosterone levels in their bloodstreams at this time of the year. Because the courtship colours of many are very bright in order to attract the attention of females, they may be more vulnerable to predation, as discussed above. Therefore, if the breeding season is limited to a small part of the year, it makes good sense to be conspicuous only at this time.

COLOUR CHANGE WITH AGE

Many young lizards are coloured differently from the adults. For instance, the bright blue tails of several skinks gradually fade as the animals mature. Another common sequence, found in geckos such as *Eublepharus macularius*, and the *Coleonyx* spp. and also in the Gila monster for instance, is for the young to be boldly banded but for these bands to fade gradually with age and be encroached upon by spots, or to break up into larger blotches. It can only be assumed that the selection pressures which exist for the young are different from those acting on the adults and so their appearance is modified accordingly. A rather special case of this involves the Kalahari lizard, *Heliobolus lugubris*, which mimics an obnoxious beetle when young but changes colour when it grows too big to be convincing (see also Chapter 5).

Where young animals are similar in colour and markings to one of the adult patterns, it is always the female which they resemble. In this case, only the males undergo a colour change when they mature. The reason for this has already been looked at: adult males are usually the more brightly coloured of the sexes and this carries a cost – females and young both 'prefer' to be camouflaged rather than flashy!

Chapter 3
Lizards
and Their Environment

The previous chapter considered how the appearance of lizards has been shaped throughout their evolutionary history by the various environmental factors acting on them. In this chapter we shall see how the environment acts on each individual during its lifetime, how that environment is perceived and how the lizard responds. 'Environment' is a fairly glib term which encompasses a whole range of factors, many of which are interconnected. Parameters such as temperature, light and humidity comprise the physical environment, while predators, prey, parasites and competitors, etc., form the biological environment. Each individual must be highly attuned to these factors, and must be capable of reacting appropriately to them if it is to survive. Some of the responses will be physiological, others will be behavioural.

THE SENSES
The first stage in responding to the environment is to be able to detect its various parameters. This is achieved by means of a variety of sense organs. Sense organs can be thought of as 'receptors'; the information they receive is 'processed' in the brain and, if action is required, this is carried out by 'effectors' such as the muscles, heart and glands.

THE EYES
Vision is the most important sense in all but a few lizard species. It is the primary means by which they find prey and avoid predators and it often plays an essential part in communication between members of a population. It is not surprising, therefore, that many lizards have good vision, although, like most animals, stationary objects are not observed as easily as moving ones. This is why captive lizards normally require live food, and why many predators rely on ambush or stealth, in order that the lizard will not notice them.

Special types of eye are found in several groups of lizards. Burrowing species may have only rudimentary eyes, sometimes covered by skin as in the blind lizards (Dibamidae) and the amphisbaenians (Plate 23). Most geckos do not have movable eyelids, neither do any of the snake lizards (pygopodids) nor night lizards (xantusids). Instead, their eyes are covered by a transparent scale, the brille, which owes its origin to the

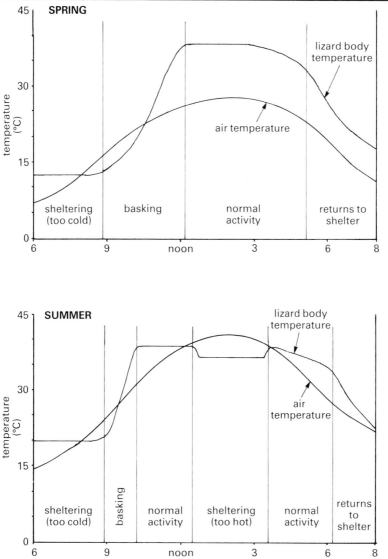

Fig. 6. Diurnal activity patterns for the same (hypothetical) lizard at different times of the year. During spring the lizard emerges late and retires early; at the height of summer its active periods may be separated by a spell of avoiding lethal temperatures by retreating beneath a rock, etc.

Thermal regulators are those species which actively attempt, by means of behavioural and physiological adaptations, to keep their body temperatures within a fairly narrow band. These species typically hide away during the night and emerge in the morning as soon as the sun appears. They may align and flatten their body in order to catch the maximum amount of radiation (Fig. 7), and some species are able to

45

Plate 27. *Agama stellio* warming itself early in the morning by clinging to a vertical surface and aligning itself to the sun's rays.

darken their coloration so that more heat is absorbed. As their body temperature reaches the preferred level, they become more active and begin to forage for food, seek mates and so on. Their body may now become paler in colour. Should the temperature continue to rise, they will seek shelter in shade or burrows; in hot parts of the world they may spend the larger part of the day in this way. If their body temperature begins to fall below the preferred level, they will return to their basking activities in order to 'top it up'. These lizards are active, diurnal species, which are characteristic of open habitats – most desert species, therefore, are thermal regulators.

Thermal conformers are species which make little or no effort to control their body temperatures but merely allow them to fluctuate up and down according to the prevailing conditions. Because of their critical minimum and maximum temperatures, however, thermal conformers can only live in regions where the climate is fairly stable, notably tropical and sub-tropical regions. Furthermore, they are usually associated with habitats where the extremes of temperature are

Fig. 7. Horned lizards (*Phrynosoma*) flatten and tilt their bodies early in the morning in order to catch the slanting rays of the sun.

46

buffered, such as below ground, in water or in constant shade. For example, the amphisbaenians, which are all burrowing reptiles, are thermal conformers, although they may be able to regulate their temperature to a small extent by moving up and down in their tunnel systems, or by moving from shaded to exposed patches of ground. Generally speaking, however, their body will be at the same temperature as the soil in which they are found.

Similarly, rain-forest lizards have little opportunity to regulate their temperature since the constant shade produced by dense vegetation allows little variation in temperature from one position to another. Most members of the huge genus *Anolis* are thought to be thermal conformers, and other forest species which also make little or no attempt to adjust their body temperatures include certain agamids and skinks. Indeed, it has been shown that under normal conditions some forest species of *Anolis* never attain their preferred body temperatures in the wild and constantly operate below them – under experimental conditions they will regularly seek and maintain higher temperatures than those at which they are found in the field. Nocturnal species, such as most geckos, also have little opportunity to regulate their temperatures, although they may be able to obtain some heat from the substrate on which they live, i.e. by convection and conduction. Often, they are most active during the evening and early part of the night when rocks, etc., still retain some of the warmth which has been absorbed from the sun during the day.

Some lizards have special problems to overcome in order to remain active for as long as possible. For instance, species living in very cold environments must be able to make good use of what little warmth is available. An extreme example of efficient thermo-regulation concerns the lava lizard, *Liolaemus multiformis*, from the Peruvian Andes. This species is black in colour and is able to absorb solar radiation so well that it can raise its body temperature to 33°C after only one hour in the sun, while the surrounding air temperature has only reached 1.5°C. In fact, this species has a preferred body temperature of 35°C, which is never reached by the air. Several other lizards from high altitudes are dark in colour and many are very rotund in shape, enabling them to conserve as much heat as possible.

A rather different problem faces the Galapagos marine iguana, *Amblyrhynchus cristatus*. This lizard lives in a hot tropical environment but must plunge into the cold water of the Humboldt Current, which surrounds its islands, in order to feed on seaweed. Under normal circumstances, its body temperature would plummet and it would rapidly be rendered helpless, but, by slowing its heart-rate to about half speed, it limits its circulation. This slows down the rate at which the cooled blood near the surface is circulated and so heat loss in the body core is considerably reduced. When the lizard comes out of the water and begins to bask again, the heart-rate returns to normal so that blood circulates through the skin rapidly, becomes warmed and carries this heat to deeper parts of the body.

In deserts, the problem is exactly reversed; here lizards face the danger of overheating and must modify their behaviour accordingly. The most important way in which they do this is to restrict their period of activity to the most appropriate time of day (which may vary throughout the year). However, this often places unreasonable limitations on the time which they can spend foraging and so on, and to counteract this they may actively keep their temperature below lethal levels by panting, and by raising their bodies up off the hot surface. In extreme cases, they raise two of their four feet in the air, alternately lifting diagonally opposed limbs. Species which must spend a lot of time foraging in the open, notably *Phrynosoma* spp. in North America and *Moloch horridus* in Australia, all of which feed exclusively on enormous quantities of ants, run a serious risk of either starvation or overheating. It has been found that these species 'compromise' by allowing their body temperature to drift upwards until it is close to lethal limits, in order to spend as much time as possible feeding.

Apart from imposing restrictions on the distribution of lizards (e.g. there are no lizards in the Arctic or Antarctic regions), temperature also

Plate 28. *Uromastyx aegypticus*, a desert-adapted agamid which rarely drinks but obtains its water by channelling moisture over its skin to its mouth. Note also the spiny tail, which discourages predators from following it down its burrow.

controls the size to which lizards can grow. Large species take much longer to warm up than small ones and so the tendency is for the largest members of each family to live nearer the equator than the medium-sized or small species. For example, all the species listed in Chapter 2 as being amongst the largest are tropical in distribution – closely related forms which live further north or south are invariably small to medium sized.

WATER BALANCE

The success of lizards in colonising deserts and other dry regions of the world has been, in part, due to their ability to avoid excessive water loss. Their scales and thick skin are relatively impermeable to water (compared to amphibians, for example). More important, they are able to excrete their waste nitrogen in the form of uric acid, which is a white crystalline substance requiring very little water to carry it out of the body. Many species are so frugal in their water requirements that they are able to obtain sufficient from their food, and need never drink.

Some desert species, such as the mastigures, *Uromastyx* spp. (Plate 28), have a highly specialised way of obtaining water from the atmosphere or from damp sand. Between their scales they have a network of fine channels arranged in such a way that water constantly moves, through capillary action, towards their mouth. They spend much of their time at the end of a deep burrow, where the substrate retains a certain amount of moisture, and their total water requirement can be obtained in this way. Other lizards, such as *Palmatogecko*, 'capture' dew on the surface of their scales and drink the droplets which condense (see also Chapter 7).

Naturally, the degree of desiccation which can be withstood depends to a very large extent on the natural habitat of the species concerned. Desert species have adapted, over millions of generations, to withstand long periods without water, but if water is withheld from rain forest lizards they will die from dehydration in a very short space of time, even at moderate temperatures.

THE CHANGING ENVIRONMENT

No matter how well evolution has moulded the anatomy, physiology and behaviour of lizards to cope with their environment, they are unable to adapt to rapid change. Although evolution is a painfully slow process, with random mutation as its driving force, it has worked admirably in the face of all the dramatic, but relatively gradual, upheavals which have occurred over the millennia.

Regrettably, the current rate of change, brought about at the hands of the human species, exceeds by far anything that evolution can respond to. In common with plants and many other animals, lizards are under threat. The delicate balance with which they interact with their physical and biotic environment is continually disturbed, and the places in which they can live are dwindling daily.

In addition, lizards are frequently killed out of superstition and ignorance, especially those which are unfortunate enough to look superficially like snakes, but also many others which, in various parts of the world, are erroneously believed to be venomous: geckos in Central America and Africa, chameleons in Africa, blue-tongued skinks in Australia, to name just a few examples.

Humans exploit lizards and also compete with them. Exploitation takes the form of hunting them for food, for skins and for the pet trade. Hunting for food is not new – lizards are relatively easy to catch, defenceless and edible, and they have always been eaten by various peoples in several parts of the world. This activity can be thought of as part of the ecology of the species, a predator–prey relationship with people as one of several predators. In fact, lizards are probably eaten less now than at any previous time, and only a few species, notably the common iguana, *Iguana iguana*, suffer at the hands of the chef. The skin trade is rather more of a problem, especially where large species, such as certain monitor lizards, are concerned, but snakes, crocodiles and non-reptilian animals bear the brunt of this abuse and controls exist to regulate the trade.

As unusual pets, lizards are steadily growing in popularity, especially in Europe and North America, where large numbers of wild-caught specimens form a significant part of the trade in exotic animals. Again, endangered species are given some degree of protection through various international laws relating to wildlife and conservation, notably the CITES recommendations. A small amount of smuggling still goes on, which is regrettable, but is unlikely to be a significant reason for the extinction of any species. Some attempts are being made to meet the demand for reptiles with captive-bred stock, but there is still a long way to go. Unfortunately, many of the most appealing species, such as chameleons, iguanas and monitors, are not easily bred in large numbers, or even kept alive for any length of time, and the demand from a largely uninformed public causes a rapid turnover; a high proportion of the animals imported last only a few months, or less, before they die through being kept under incorrect conditions. Set against this, the educational value of captive lizards, whether in zoos or private collections, undoubtedly contributes much towards public awareness of conservation issues. The situation would be improved by an effort to educate would-be keepers and breeders, and to direct their attention towards common species which tolerate confinement well and which breed readily in captivity.

All the above factors, important though they are for certain species, pale into insignificance when compared with the effect that the human race as 'competitor' is having. The explosion of the human population, with its hunger for land and resources, is rapidly destroying, for ever, the numerous habitats which lizards and other animals need. The remaining areas of rain forest, grassland and deserts are being fragmented to such an extent that populations are becoming first isolated, then exterminated. Conservation laws, which are often effective in protecting individual animals from individual persons, are no obstacle to land-development, military activities and pollution.

A few species may benefit temporarily from human activities – settlements often attract thriving populations of adaptable species, such as house geckos which capitalise on the rich new source of flies, cockroaches and other insects, while forest clearings become corridors of dispersal for species which require open habitats and a sunny microhabitat (at the cost of specialised forest species which they oust or eat). Artificial habitats, such as dry stone walls in southern Europe, provide numerous territories and refuges for rock-dwelling species, such as wall lizards and geckos, and often boost populations artificially.

Protection is deservedly given to species which are especially vulnerable or especially interesting, or both, but species which are common are often given no protection whatsoever, at least until they cease to be common and therefore become interesting!

The list on page 52, which is taken from the IUCN Red List of Threatened Animals, shows which species have been pinpointed as requiring legal protection because of exploitation, habitat destruction or other causes. Unfortunately, it is necessarily selective – many species which are in imminent danger of extinction go unnoticed, usually because they come from parts of the world where the necessities of life do not extend to the study of wild animals which have no economic importance.

It is worth noting that a very high proportion of these species live on islands. Although lizards have been remarkably successful in colonising islands, as described in Chapter 7, the populations which have evolved there are very prone to extinction at the hands of humans and,

Plate 29. *Cyclura cornuta*, the rhinoceros iguana, is one of several large ground iguanas from the West Indies which are seriously threatened with extinction.

especially, human introductions in the form of domestic cats, rats, pigs and goats. Island ecosystems are extremely fragile ones which quickly show the effects of human impact, and are good indicators of the effects of ecological disturbance on lizards.

(i) Endangered species

Phelsuma edwardnewtonii	Rodrigues day gecko	Indian Ocean
Anolis roosvelti	Culebra giant anole	Puerto Rico
Brachylophus fasciatus	Fiji banded iguana	Fiji, Tonga
Cyclura pinguis	Anegada ground iguana	Virgin Islands
Gambelia silus	San Joaquin leopard lizard	USA
Gallotia simonyi	Hierro giant lizard	Canary Islands
Ameiva polops	St Croix ground lizard	Virgin Islands
Anniella pulchra nigra	Black legless lizard	USA

(ii) Vulnerable species

Oedura reticulata	Reticulated gecko	Australia
Hydrosaurus pustulatus	Sail-fin lizard	Philippines
Conolophus subcristatus	Galapagos land iguana	Galapagos Is.
Cyclura nubila	Cuban ground iguana	Cuba
Cnemidophorus hyperythrus	Orange-throated whiptail	Mexico, USA
Heloderma suspectum	Gila monster	Mexico, USA
Varanus griseus caspius	Central Asian monitor	Asia

(iii) Rare species

Cyrtodactylus serensinsula	Serpent Island gecko	Indian Ocean
Phelsuma guentheri	Round Island day gecko	Indian Ocean
Xantusia riversiana	Island night lizard	USA
Amblyrhynchus cristatus	Marine iguana	Galapagos Is.
Conolophus pallidus	Barrington land iguana	Galapagos Is.
Cyclura carinata	Turks & Caicos iguana	West Indies
Cyclura cyclura	Andros ground iguana	West Indies
Podarcis f. filfolensis	Filfola wall lizard	Malta
Gongylomorphus bojerii	Macab forest skink	Indian Ocean
Leiolopisma telfairii	Round Island skink	Indian Ocean
Varanus komodoensis	Komodo dragon	Indonesia

(iv) Threatened or status unknown

Cyclura cornuta	Rhinoceros iguana	West Indies
Cyclura ricordii	Hispaniola ground iguana	West Indies
Cyclura rileyi	Riley's ground iguana	West Indies
Phrynosoma cornutum blainvillei	San Diego horned lizard	USA
Macroscincus coctaei	Cape Verde giant skink	Cape Verde Is.
Gerrhonotus panamintus	Panamint alligator lizard	USA
Heloderma horridum	Beaded lizard	Mexico, Guatemala

Chapter 4
Food and Feeding

TYPES OF FOOD

Collectively, lizards show a wide range of variation in their dietary requirements. Some species are remarkably catholic in taste, and will eat almost anything organic into which they can get their teeth, but other species are highly specialised and feed only on one or two types of prey. The degree of specialisation depends to some extent on the richness of the habitat in which they live. Thus, many lizards which live in regions where the range of flora and fauna is not wide, for instance on small islands or in the desert, are more adaptable regarding their diet than those living in habitats where food is more plentiful. This is one aspect of a process known as 'niche separation'. In a favourable area there are likely to be many species of lizards, each of which specialises so that it can exploit a particular source of food to the full. If food is in short supply, however, there are likely to be fewer species of lizards and each can utilise a wider range of the food, i.e. it has a broader niche.

The pygopodids (snake lizards) are mostly insectivorous, but at least one species, *Lialis burtoni*, Burton's snake lizard, feeds largely on other lizards, especially skinks, and another, *Pygopus nigriceps*, eats mostly scorpions. The closely related geckos are all insectivorous as far as is known, although large species, such as the tokay, *Gekko gecko*, will tackle small rodents and smaller species of lizards given the opportunity. The night lizards are usually regarded as insectivores, although it is known that some of the species also include plant material in their diet, and one species, *Xantusia riversiana*, which is restricted to a few small islands off the coast of southern California, probably relies heavily on this material in order to survive in its relatively barren environment.

Among the iguanids, there is a strong correlation between size and diet. Whereas the smaller species, such as the spiny lizards, *Sceloporus* (Plate 30) and the *Anolis* spp., etc., are mostly insectivorous, the larger ones, such as the common iguana, *Iguana iguana*, the chuckwalla, *Sauromalus obesus*, the Fiji iguanas, *Brachylophus* (Plate 31), and the rhinoceros iguanas, *Cyclura* spp., are herbivores, although they may also take some insects, especially when young.

Species which are intermediate in size, such as the collared and leopard lizards, *Crotaphytus* (Plate 32) and *Gambelia*, often prey upon smaller species of lizards, although their diets are not restricted to them. Some iguanids are extreme specialists. For instance, lizards of the genus *Dracaena*, the caiman lizards, feed only on molluscs. The 14 species of horned lizards, *Phrynosoma* spp., of North and Central America, feed largely on ants, although they will also eat other insects. The Galapagos marine iguana, *Amblyrhynchus cristatus*, has one of the most unusual diets

Plate 30. Western fence lizard, *Sceloporus occidentalis,* a typical small insectivorous iguanid.

of all lizards; it feeds exclusively on marine algae (seaweed) which it grazes from the seabed, diving beneath the surface for extended periods of time in order to feed. The only other large iguanid with which it shares its archipelago, the Galapagos land iguana, *Conolophus subcristatus,* is also a vegetarian, but it feeds on terrestrial plants, particularly the fleshy leaves and fruit of *Opuntia* cacti (prickly pear). It deals with the long spines by working the plant material around in its tough mouth until they have all been broken off.

The agamids are mostly insectivores, although the mastigures, *Uromastyx* spp., from North Africa and the Middle East eat plant material, perhaps exclusively, and at least some of the bearded dragons, *Pogona,* will also eat vegetable material. *Moloch horridus,* the Australian thorny devil, eats only ants of the genus *Iridomyrmex,* taking up to 2,500 individuals at a sitting. Chameleons are also insectivores, but some of the larger species are quite capable of catching and eating smaller lizards, birds and mammals. In captivity, they frequently eat young of their own species, perhaps as a result of unnaturally crowded conditions. The teiids eat insects, larger animals

54

food during the birds' breeding season is sufficient to sustain the lizards for the rest of the year.

The zonures and plated lizards are mostly insectivorous, but one species, *Angolosaurus skoogi*, which lives in the Namib Desert, probably relies heavily on seeds and other plant debris which are blown from the coastal grasslands and forests onto the dunes where it lives. Again, some of the large species, such as the plated lizards, *Gerrhosaurus validus* and *G. major*, also take plant material, especially fallen fruits and berries. The anguids, especially the European slow-worm and other legless forms, are well known for their preference for slugs and snails, but these and other species eat a wide variety of other food, such as insects, young rodents and smaller lizards. The crocodile lizard, *Shinisaurus*, eats insects, but, in keeping with its semi-aquatic life-style, also takes small fish and tadpoles.

The Gila monster and beaded lizard are carnivores, but include many items in their diet. Due to their ponderous locomotion, they are rarely able to catch fast-moving prey, and are therefore restricted to nestling rodents, rabbits and hares, and to the eggs of ground-nesting birds, such as those of Gambel's quail, a common desert species. There are also reports of Gila monsters congregating in areas beneath the burrows of cliff-nesting birds in order to cash in on the dead and dying young which occasionally fall to the ground during the breeding season.

The prey of monitor lizards reflects their size range. The smaller species, often known collectively as 'pygmy' monitors, feed largely on insects and small lizards. Species of intermediate size, e.g. *Varanus eremius* and *V. tristis*, also eat lizards and rather less insects, while a number of species are arboreal, searching for nestling birds and mammals in hollow trees. The large species will readily accept any animal material which they can catch, as well as carrion. The Nile monitor, *V. niloticus*, is well known for its liking for eggs, including those of crocodiles, which it obtains by raiding nests, and the Asian water monitor, *V. salvator*, also hunts for turtle nests on beaches (Plate 34). The huge Komodo dragon, *V. komodoensis*, may subsist largely on carrion, although it is capable of attacking and bringing down animals up to the size of small deer. Since becoming a tourist attraction, its diet has been supplemented by dead domestic animals, generously provided by the tourists in order to entice the lizards into the viewfinders of their cameras. It has also, on at least three occasions, added the tourists themselves to its diet.

HUNTING METHODS

The strategies which lizards use to obtain their food are largely dependent on the type of food they eat. Obviously, herbivorous species are obliged to forage actively for suitable material to eat, whereas species which feed on insects and other animals have two options open to them: they can sit and wait for their food to blunder by, or they can go in search of it. Most insectivorous species probably do a little of each – if ' presents itself while they are resting or basking they will gratefully

Plate 34. An Asian water monitor, *Varanus salvator*, digging up turtle eggs on a beach in Sri Lanka. (Photograph courtesy of Stephen Peltz.)

snap it up, but they also devote some time and energy to visiting sites, e.g. flowering plants, etc., where insects are likely to congregate. With specialised prey, the hunting strategy is dependent on the habits of that prey. For instance, species which feed on scorpions or other nocturnal animals can either search them out when they are resting in their daytime retreats, or attempt to ambush them at night when they themselves are foraging.

A similar situation exists with the species which prey on other lizards; sit-and-wait predators feed mainly on the lizards which actively forage, whereas other lizards actively forage for the ones which are sitting and waiting!

Most insectivorous lizards are fast-moving and agile and are able snails. Two small lizards from New Zealand, a gecko and a skink, occasionally enter shallow water in order to catch mosquito larvae, and in the New World at least three species of *Anolis*, *A. lionotus*, *A. poecilopus* and *A. barkeri*, catch a sizeable proportion of their food in the water. No doubt numerous other species of lizards take the odd insect from the surface of water, but few appear to specialise in this method of hunting.

Little is known of the feeding behaviour of the amphisbaenians or fossorial lizards, although it is assumed that they generally eat burrowing invertebrates such as earthworms, beetle larvae, etc. The Mexican *Bipes biporus* seems to eat mainly termites and their larvae, and is commonly found in the soil surrounding old fence posts and other wooden structures around which the termite colonies are centred. In captivity this species has also been observed suddenly breaking through the surface of the sand in order to grasp small lizards. For this to be possible, it must be highly sensitive to the vibrations of small animals walking across the substrate while it lies in wait just beneath the surface. At least one gecko, *Gehyra pilbara*, has so far been found only in termite mounds. This close association may not be entirely due to the lizard's diet preferences, as other factors (such as a suitable egg-laying site) may be involved.

Herbivorous lizards have little need for speed and agility, save the need to escape from possible predators. Quite a few of them are large, and well protected by spines or thick scales, which provide some protection while they are feeding. Many herbivorous lizards have characteristically blunt snouts, for example the mastigures, which are adapted to grazing (in fact, the shape of their heads is similar to those of tortoises, which occupy similar niches).

PREY-HANDLING

The vast majority of lizards, whether herbivorous or carnivorous, merely find their food, grasp it and swallow it. Several species, having caught their prey, shake it vigorously, sometimes bashing it against a rock or on the ground in order to subdue it. Others chew repeatedly on their victim, often working it backwards and forwards until it is well and truly crushed. Where large food items are eaten, they may be turned around in the mouth until they are in the most convenient position to be swallowed – usually head-first.

Few lizards are as efficient at capturing their food as the chameleons. Despite their ponderous gait, chameleons stalk and catch enormous numbers of insects, small reptiles, mammals and birds by means of their extendable tongue. When a chameleon sights potential prey, it begins to move towards it in its typically slow and deliberate manner, frequently using one of its eyes to look over its shoulder for possible danger. As soon as it is within range, both eyes are focused on the prey and the head is accurately aligned, so that when the muscular tongue is shot out it hits the prey squarely. The tip of the tongue is covered with sticky mucus to trap the prey, which is then drawn rapidly into the mouth and crushed.

Chapter 5
Defence

Lizards form an important link in many food-chains. Although most of them are predatory, they, in turn, are preyed upon by an assortment of larger predators. These include many carnivorous mammals and birds and a large number of snakes, many of which are out and out lizard specialists. In addition, small lizards are frequently eaten by larger lizards (see previous chapter).

Defence strategies have evolved along several lines. A good way of not being eaten is not to be noticed. Once noticed, the next best thing is to try not to be caught, or to look as unappetising as possible. However, predators also have to survive and they, in turn, become experts at finding, catching and overpowering their prey. The predator–prey relationship therefore develops into a kind of arms race, with both parties constantly up-dating their techniques just to stay in the game.

CRYPSIS
Like most animals, lizards' main line of defence is to avoid detection, either by hiding or by relying on their camouflage. Most species are coloured in such a way as to match their surroundings, and, even within species, this may vary from place to place according to the local conditions. For example, lesser earless lizards, *Holbrookia maculata*, which live in the drier parts of southern North America, are normally brown in colour and therefore well camouflaged when resting or moving through dead vegetation or over rocks, but the population which lives among the gypsum dunes found in parts of New Mexico are almost pure white in colour (Plate 37).

Plate 37. The population of lesser earless lizards living around White Sands, New Mexico, have evolved an almost pure white coloration in order to be well camouflaged against the unusual substrate on which they live. Elsewhere the species is grey or brownish.

Fig. 8.

Plate 38. The Australian leaf-tailed gecko, *Phyllurus cornutus,* is a master of camouflage. The accompanying figure shows the outline of the lizard.

Plain camouflage is not common, however, since few substrates are uniformly coloured. Therefore, the majority of lizards have markings which consist of blotches, stripes or bands, and these help to break up the animal's outline and cause its image to merge into the background. This is known as disruptive coloration and is common throughout the animal kingdom. It is a technique often borrowed by humans for use in a military context. Many of the illustrations show lizards which are disruptively coloured, but Plate 38, of a large arboreal gecko from Australia (*Phyllurus cornutus*), shows just how astonishingly effective this type of camouflage can be. Patterns consisting of longitudinal stripes running along the back and onto the tail (Plate 52) may also be disruptive, but are probably more effective when the lizard is fleeing –

under these circumstances the stripes cause the eye to be deceived, making it difficult to keep the lizard in sight or to know which part of the body to attack.

Some species are shaped and coloured in such a way as to resemble an inanimate object. Examples of this include chameleons, which are extremely flattened, and coloured to resemble the leaves among which they live. They exploit this disguise further by moving slowly with a swaying gait, and by tending to move only when a breeze is ruffling the vegetation. The spiny Australian agamid, *Moloch horridus*, freezes when it is approached, and raises its tail in the air, making itself resemble one of the small thorny plants which grow in its desert environment. Other species merely crouch close to the ground or lie along branches or twigs in order to escape detection and no doubt this technique works in many cases, since lizards are only easily seen when they move suddenly. In some cases, these species flatten themselves to the substrate, and this technique is useful in preventing the shadow which would otherwise be cast. Shadow elimination is an especially important technique to species which live on pale substrates and in bright sunlight; however well they match their surroundings, a sharply defined black shadow will quickly give them away to a hungry predator. Such species will only raise their bodies off the substrate in order to display, or when they dart from place to place. In extreme cases, frills and flaps have been evolved, and these act like cloaks to even out the irregularities in the lizard's outline and soften or disguise its shadow.

ESCAPE

If a lizard is detected, either because its camouflage is not effective, or because its movements have been spotted, it will usually resort to flight. Although they are unable to move rapidly over long distances, lizards usually live and forage within a well-defined area which contains one or more retreats. Escape then takes the form of a rapid dash to this retreat, although they may pause once or more en route. The type of retreat depends largely upon the habitat in which the lizard is living.

Species which live in open areas often dig burrows in which they shelter during unfavourable conditions. In arid parts of North America, the common iguanid, *Uta stansburiana*, often sets up home around the base of a small shrub, such as a creosote bush. It constructs a burrow in the sand around the roots of the bush and its home range is centred on this burrow. It rarely ventures more than a few feet from the entrance to the burrow and runs back towards it at the first hint of danger. If the entrance to the burrow is blocked, the lizard will continually attempt to find its way in rather than leaving its 'home bush' (Fig. 9). In Australian deserts, a variety of small lizards use clumps of spinifex grass in the same way. Several of the species which live in burrows have heavily armoured tails which they use to block the entrance, so avoiding the possibility of further pursuit. Examples include the mastigures, *Uromastix* spp., and the giant zonure, *Cordylus giganteus*. On a smaller scale, the tiny

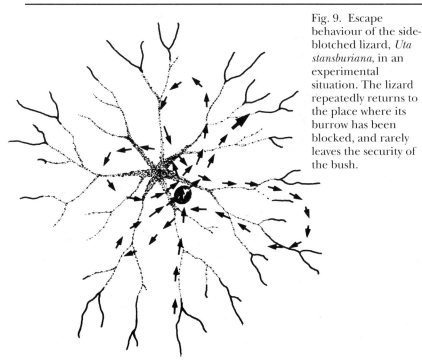

Fig. 9. Escape behaviour of the side-blotched lizard, *Uta stansburiana*, in an experimental situation. The lizard repeatedly returns to the place where its burrow has been blocked, and rarely leaves the security of the bush.

Australian gecko, *Diplodactylus conspicillatus*, apparently hides in disused spider burrows – the diameter of its bulbous tail is wider than its body and effectively blocks the burrow (although this strategy may also be connected with water conservation).

Species which dwell among rocks and outcrops, for instance the African rock lizards of the genera *Pseudocordylus* and *Platysaurus*, and the granite night lizard, *Xantusia henshawi* (Plate 85), from North America, are often dorsally flattened, so that they can squeeze into narrow crevices. Other rock-dwelling species, such as the crevice spiny lizard, *Sceloporus poinsetti*, the Australian skinks, *Egernia depressa* and *E. stokesii*, and several of the Andean species of the iguanid genus *Leiocephalus*, have spiny tails which they may curl around in front of their bodies, protecting them from attack, while others, such as the chuckwalla, *Sauromalus obesus*, inflate their bodies with air, making it practically impossible to dislodge them.

There are relatively very few aquatic lizards, but those which do exist obviously use water as their main line of escape, either swimming through it or diving to the bottom and hiding temporarily beneath rocks or debris. The European lacertid, *Lacerta screiberi*, which often lives alongside streams, may occasionally resort to this strategy, although in doing so it runs the risk of becoming torpid due to the low temperature of the water, and therefore vulnerable if followed. The ability of basilisk lizards to run across the surface of water has already been referred to, but other related species, notably the common iguana, *Iguana iguana*,

Plate 39. The typical basking or resting position of the Asian water dragon, on a branch overhanging a river or lake.

the Asian water dragons, *Physignathus* (Plate 39), and the sail-fin lizards, *Hydrosaurus*, may bask on branches overhanging rivers and drop to the water if approached.

'Swimming' through sand is a fairly common tactic in species which live among dunes. Lizards such as *Uma notata* in North America and its West African counterparts, *Aporosaura anchietae* and *Angolosaurus skoogi*, which live in the Namib Desert, run for a short distance across the sand and then dive beneath the surface to escape. Several species of skinks are even more specialised. These 'sandfish' have smooth scales and rudimentary limbs, or limbs which are absent altogether, and move quickly through loose sand by means of a rapid undulatory motion (Plate 5), and the two small *Anniella* species from south-western North America are so totally adapted to this means of locomotion that they are found only in dunes of fine sand, usually in coastal regions. If any of these species are placed on the surface of dry sand, they disappear from view immediately, and there is no doubt that sand-swimming is a most effective way of escaping from predators.

Arboreal or semi-arboreal species climb into higher branches, and may make an effort to move around to the opposite side of the trunk. Others move into the densest parts of thorny vegetation. Chameleons, which are incapable of rapid movement, have a disconcerting habit of

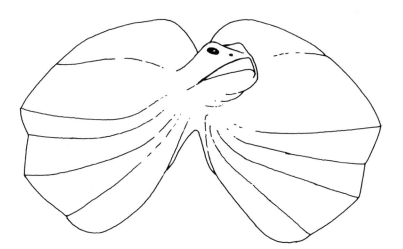

Fig. 10. The frilled lizard, *Chlamydosaurus kingii*, spreads its ruff if threatened, making itself appear larger and more fierce.

the scales to protrude (Plate 45). Still in Australia, the blue-tongued skinks, forming part of the genus *Tiliqua*, have, as their common name implies, a bright blue tongue which is thrust out of the open mouth if they are molested.

BLOOD-SQUIRTING

Three species of horned lizards (*Phrynosoma cornutum, coronatum* and *solare*) have a strange and unique defence mechanism. If their camouflage and intimidation strategies do not work, they are able to increase the blood pressure in the sinuses of the eye-sockets until the walls burst. The blood which is released then flows beneath the eyelids, which are kept closed, and eventually emerges as a thin stream through pores in the lower eyelids. It appears that certain predators find the taste of the blood unpleasant and will abandon their attack on the lizard if squirted in the mouth or eyes. The stream of blood may have a range of up to 122 cm (4 ft) and may be repeated several times.

MIMICRY

Mimicry is a defence strategy which is well known among insects, fish and other animals, but has not been exploited to any great extent by lizards. Only one definite example is documented, although there are several other possible cases, all of which are interesting. A lacertid lizard from the Kalahari desert in Africa, *Heliobolus lugubris*, while juvenile, is a Batesian mimic of an unpalatable species of beetle from the same region. Both the beetle and the young lizard are boldly marked in black and white, and the lizard further enhances the similarity by walking stiff-legged with an arched back. Its tail is reddish, matching the ground, and is held low so that it does not spoil the illusion. Since only half-grown lizards approximate to the size of the beetles, they eventually grow out of their mimetic option. At this stage they lose the bold markings and become camouflaged like the adults.

At least three species of snake lizards (Pygopodidae) from Australia are thought to mimic venomous snakes. Obviously, these lizards start off with a large advantage in not possessing legs, but the species *Delma fraseri* and *D. impar* appear to mimic juvenile brown snakes, *Demansia textilis*, and *Pygopus nigriceps* may also mimic one or more species of *Denisonia*. In all three of these species, mimetic behaviour, consisting of raising the head and inflating the neck region in the same way as the snakes concerned, is employed in addition to a similarity of markings.

The other case of mimicry is poorly documented, but concerns the gecko *Teratolepsis fasciata*, which shares its habitat in Pakistan with the dangerously venomous saw-scaled viper, *Echis carinatus*. The tail of the gecko is supposed to resemble the head of the viper and, if disturbed, it apparently moves it in such a way as to enhance the illusion.

Plate 41. *Eumeces fasciatus* from North America, one of several skinks which have a bright blue tail, the purpose of which is to attract the attention of a predator. This deflects the attack away from the head and body, and the tail can be discarded if necessary.

TAIL-LOSS

The ability to discard all or part of the tail is widespread among lizards. This process, known as autotomy, is well developed in the geckos, skinks, lacertids, teiids and anguids, but also occurs in several other families and is completely unknown in only five families (Chamaeleonidae, Helodermatidae, Varanidae, Lanthonotidae and Xenosauridae). The breakage occurs across a definite fracture-plane which is found on several of the caudal vertebrae. Associated with each fracture plane are special muscles, which cause the tail to part from the body and continue to wriggle (and so hold the predator's interest), and structures for closing down the blood vessels so that blood-loss is minimised. A replacement tail begins to grow immediately after tail-loss, although the regrown tail is usually different in markings to the original, and is supported by cartilage rather than bone vertebrae. In lizards, but not in some amphisbaenians, there is no limit to the number of times a regrown tail can be automised.

Readiness to part with the tail is dependent to some extent on the lizard's life-style. Some species are so free and easy with their tails that it is almost impossible to find an example with an original one, but species

Plate 42. An unidentified teiid from Ecuador has an almost identical coloration to the skink in Plate 41, undoubtedly evolved for exactly the same purpose.

Plate 43. A number of geckos, such as this Asian ground gecko, have a boldly banded tail to deflect the attack of a predator. If threatened, the tail is often raised and waved slowly about.

which live in a harsh environment often use the tail to store fat reserves, and these lizards may be reluctant to sacrifice such an important organ. For some strange reason, however, it has been noted that those which do autotomise often re-grow a thicker tail the second time around. There may also be variation within individuals; when a lizard is cold, it is less able to run away and may therefore be willing to discard its tail more readily. Usually the tail only breaks off when it is grasped by a predator, but under certain circumstances some species voluntarily autotomise. Autotomy may also result from intra-specific fighting; the frequency of regrown tails is higher in the males of some species than in females (although this may also be because, in many species, males are more conspicuous and active than females and therefore more likely to be attacked).

Since this can be such an effective survival tactic, it is not surprising that certain lizards go out of their way to encourage predators to attack their tail rather than more vulnerable parts of their body, and in these species the tail is brightly coloured. Several species of skinks, lacertids and teiids (Plates 41 and 42) have brilliant blue tails, while in other species the tail is boldly marked with black and white bands, as in the gecko illustrated in Plate 43. When they are threatened, these species wriggle the tail enticingly, sometimes raising it above their back. It is usual in these species for the tails of the juveniles to be more vivid than those of the adults, and in several cases the tail gradually takes on the normal, camouflaged, coloration as the animal matures – obviously, the size of juveniles makes them more vulnerable to predation.

Lizards which lose their tail may live to fight another day, but there are several costs involved. Re-growing another tail can be expensive in terms of energy, and young lizards which discard their tail do not grow as rapidly as others which have not. Similarly, females which lose their tail lay fewer eggs, and sometimes fail to breed altogether. Finally, the tail acts as an important counterbalance in some lizards, especially those which run on their back legs, and losing the tail can reduce their maximum speed by up to 40 per cent.

An interesting spin-off is the way in which some predators exploit autotomy. Some small snakes are thought to feed largely on the broken tails of lizards, as do the small monitors *Varanus gilleni* and *V. caudolineatus*. Even more bizarre is the habit, noted in the skinks *Lygosoma* and *Ctenotus*, of returning to the spot where they lost their tails and eating them, a unique case of self-cannibalism!

Amongst amphisbaenians, caudal autotomy appears to be common, although it is not an ability shared by all species. A fundamental difference between amphisbaenid and lizard autotomy is that the tail, once lost, is not re-grown. It is therefore a 'once and for all' strategy, but is nevertheless most useful, judging from the high proportion of specimens which are found with a damaged tail. Certain of these burrowing reptiles suffer predation at the hands of specialist predators, especially coral snakes, which track them along their tunnels. The shedding of the end segment of tail is therefore an important defence because this will effectively plug the tunnel until the snake has eaten it. Furthermore, since coral snakes are highly venomous, there may be some protection to be gained by discarding the bitten portion and thereby isolating the venom from the rest of the system.

MISCELLANEOUS STRATEGIES

The possession of a boldly marked tail is mentioned above in connection with caudal autotomy, as is the consideration that tail-loss can be disastrous for those species which use the tail as a counterbalance when running. An alternative explanation for a banded tail has been proposed for the agile North American iguanids belonging to the genera *Uma*, *Cophosaurus* and *Callisaurus*. These species have broad black bands on the underside of their long tails (*Callisaurus draconoides* is known as the zebra-tailed lizard). If any of these lizards see a possible predator, they raise their tails, thus exposing the eye-catching pattern, then run a few yards, stop, and then perhaps repeat the sequence. It seems unlikely that these lizards are encouraging predators to attack, since they are rarely found with regrown tails, and an alternative explanation is that raising the tail constitutes a signal to the predator, sending a message which reads, 'You've been spotted – I can run away so don't waste your time stalking me.' The advantages of this strategy are that the predator, knowing that it has little chance of catching the lizard, loses interest and the lizard can continue its activities without having to expend energy by running away. A predator would soon learn what the signal means after one or two fruitless attempts to catch an alerted lizard.

Plate 44. The zebra-tailed lizard, *Callisaurus draconoides,* in a typical posture in the Mojave Desert. When approached, the lizard raises its tail, showing the black and white stripes on its underside, before running a short distance. This may tell an approaching predator that it has been spotted and has little chance of catching the lizard, a signal which saves both parties from expending valuable energy.

Plate 45. A bearded dragon, *Pogona vitticeps,* displaying its 'beard' and the brightly coloured inside of its mouth in response to disturbance.

Chapter 6

Reproduction

The way in which lizards breed often reflects their life-style and social behaviour as well as their taxonomic relationships. Courtship and mating often involve elaborate and colourful displays, more analogous to birds than to other kinds of reptiles, while their reproductive methods have been moulded by evolutionary necessity to encompass a wide range of strategies.

BREEDING SEASONS
Most lizards breed at a certain time of the year, although this season may consist of a fairly extended period. Each breeding season has evolved in such a way that when the young are born or hatched, they have the best possible chance of survival. In temperate regions, with a warm summer and cold winter, mating usually commences almost as soon as the animals emerge from hibernation, although some species, such as the skink, *Eumeces copei*, may mate before they enter hibernation, the sperm being stored until the following spring when delayed fertilisation takes place. Either way, development of the eggs or young takes place in the spring or early summer; the young appear well before the onset of cold weather and are able to feed for the maximum amount of time before they have to hibernate. In this case, the urge to breed is brought on by a combination of gradually increasing daylength and rising temperatures.

In other regions, the breeding season may coincide with a wet season or a dry season, depending on the requirements of the lizards, and here rainfall may control breeding. However, in these species there will still be a certain 'permissive' minimum temperature below which they will not breed regardless of other conditions. Rainfall and other seasonal factors may act directly or through other linked factors such as food supply – this aspect of breeding biology is difficult to investigate and there may be other important considerations of which we are not yet aware.

In cold climates, the breeding season may last only long enough for the females to lay one clutch of eggs (or give birth to one brood of young) each year (all British species are so restricted) and, in extreme cases, females may lay only every other year. However, if the period of suitable conditions lasts throughout most of the year, each female may lay repeatedly. This occurs in areas such as the Mediterranean region and the warmer parts of North America, southern Africa, etc., where small species may lay three or four clutches of eggs each year. In species which have a wide geographical or altitudinal range, they may be variation between one population and another, one set laying several clutches during a season and the other laying only one or two. Finally, in tropical regions, lizards may breed continuously throughout the year. This does not necessarily mean that each female breeds many times every year – if the species is large, each may lay only once or twice – but their breeding cycle will not be synchronised and young from different females may be hatching at different times.

COURTSHIP

Many lizards are diurnal, visually orientated animals, which rely heavily on colour and display to identify themselves and to attract mates. Because male competition and combat are often important stages in the 'right' to mate, males of many species are larger and more brightly coloured than the females, and they may be decorated with flamboyant crests, horns or other appendages. In some cases, this courtship coloration is only present, or at least intensified, during the breeding season (probably due to increased levels of the sex hormone testosterone at this time of the year), while in other species the advertisement colours are kept hidden (to avoid predation) until the lizard displays. Good examples of this include the many species of *Anolis*, which lower throat fans during their displays, and a number of small iguanids, cordylids, etc., which have brightly coloured throats and undersides which are exposed when the lizard raises itself up on its legs (Fig. 12).

Plate 46. Male and female *Gonatodes vittatus* from Trinidad. Sexual dimorphism is common among diurnal lizards, with the males nearly always being brighter than the females.

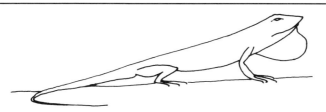

Fig. 11. Male *Anolis* species lower their brightly coloured dewlaps in order to attract the attention of other individuals. The sequence of flicks, and the head-bobbing which accompanies them, is unique to each species and therefore acts as an isolating mechanism.

Most lizard displays are stereotyped, consisting of head-bobbing and/or 'push-ups' in a fixed sequence which serves to identify each species and so avoid hybridisation. Males typically display in a prominent position such as a rock, termite mound or tree-trunk, the exact nature of which obviously depends on their habitat. Neighbouring males are thus warned that the territory is occupied, and will be challenged if they approach, usually by intensified displaying and chasing. Under certain circumstances, physical combat may ensue. By the same means, receptive females are advised of the presence and eligibility of the male and may approach in order to be mated. Although the social structure of lizards is not well understood, and varies between species anyway, it appears that males often operate a kind of harem system, in which a number of females live within a territory controlled by a single male, as in the chuckwallas, *Sauromalus* spp. Juvenile males are usually coloured in the same way as the females, so that their presence will be tolerated in a territory by adult males until they mature.

Geckos and pygopods (snake lizards) provide an interesting

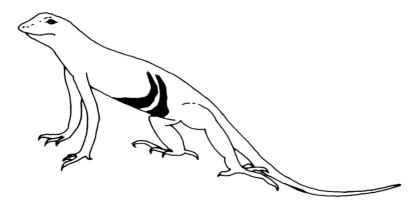

Fig. 12. Male earless lizards, as well as certain other species of iguanids and agamids, raise their bodies in a series of push-ups in order to show the bright flash coloration on their flanks. At other times they crouch, hiding the markings and maintaining their cryptic coloration.

Plate 47. *Anolis sagrei*, the Cuban anole, displaying its bright orange throat-fan in suburban surroundings.

Plate 48. *Cophosaurus texana*, the greater earless lizard, is well camouflaged except when it displays the colour flashes on its flanks by raising its body off the ground.

departure from this system. Many are nocturnal and therefore have no use for visual display, and so they vocalise in order to announce their status and whereabouts. Males are highly territorial and will react aggressively to calls from the same species. However, a minority of species *are* diurnal, such as the day geckos, *Phelsuma*, from Madagascar and the Indian Ocean region. These are brightly coloured, often exceedingly so, and they employ display sequences involving head-bobbing and tail-waving.

Unfortunately, what we know about lizard mating and courtship behaviour is based largely on observations of the more conspicuous species. Lizards which spend much of their time hidden away, such as the burrowing species, are little known in this respect and much research will be needed before we begin to understand the systems which operate.

MATING

Mating is achieved by the male twisting his tail beneath that of the female, everting one of his hemipenes, and transferring his sperm directly into the female's cloaca. In many species the male uses his jaws to grasp the female behind the head and females often show scars in this region, resulting from the rough and tumble of mating. Several matings may occur over a period of days or even weeks but, as mentioned above, the sperm may not fertilise the female's eggs immediately and can be stored for up to several months.

DEVELOPMENT

Within the lizards there is a complete spectrum of reproductive methods with oviparity (egg-laying) and viviparity (live birth) at either extreme. Thus, some species lay eggs in which the embryo has barely started to develop, others lay eggs which are almost at the point of hatching or which hatch immediately prior to laying (ovo-viviparity), while some are truly viviparous in that the embryo is closely connected to the female by a placenta and derives nourishment from her thoughout its development and growth.

Five families of lizards, the geckos, night lizards, anguids, lacertids and skinks, contain truly viviparous (as opposed to ovo-viviparous) species. However, in none of these families are all members viviparous, and the evolution of viviparity is strongly connected with the climatic conditions under which some of these species live. For example, species belonging to the genus *Elgaria* (previously known as *Gerrhonotus*) are called alligator lizards. Two of these species live along the west coast of North America. The northern species, *E. coeruleus*, which lives in a cool climate, gives birth to live young, whereas the southern species, *E. multicarinatus*, lays eggs. Similarly, of the European lizards belonging to the genus *Lacerta*, all are egg-layers except *L. vivipara*, the common lizard, which occurs further north than any of the others, ranging right

Plate 49. The European common lizard, *Lacerta vivipara*, is unique in its family in being viviparous. This strategy has evolved to counteract the cold environment in which the species lives.

into the Arctic Circle in Scandinavia. A final example concerns the skinks of the genus *Eumeces*. Here, the three species which give birth to live young, *E. copei*, *E. dicei* and *E. lynxe*, are from Mexico, whereas the oviparous species extend well up into North America – this would seem to be contrary to the above rule, but the important factor here is altitude – all three are montane species.

The connection between cool conditions and viviparity stems from the fact that the speed of development is controlled by temperature – eggs which are kept cool develop much more slowly than those which are kept warm. By retaining the embryos inside her body, a female living in a cool climate can move about according to the direction of the sun and wind to create the warmest possible conditions for her developing offspring. This strategy has enabled lizards to move into areas of the northerly or southerly latitudes or of high altitude, which would have been unavailable to them if they were forced to depend on the vagaries of the weather to incubate their eggs. On the other hand, if the climate *is* warm enough to allow the eggs to be buried and left, so much the better – the female is not hindered by the extra burden of developing young inside her body and finds it easier to escape from predators and hunt for food. Furthermore, by 'dumping' her eggs as soon as possible she may be able to begin forming a subsequent clutch straightaway and so increase her production for the season.

Because of temperature variations, the incubation times of lizard eggs are not constant, but are typically one to two months in length.

EGG-LAYING

With the exception of most of the geckos and pygopods, which lay hard-shelled eggs (rather like spherical birds' eggs), oviparous lizards secrete a leathery shell around their eggs. The shell is permeable to water and so it is important that it is not laid in too dry a place or the egg will lose water and the embryo will die. (In fact, most lizard eggs take up water throughout their development.) Females therefore find a moist place in which to lay their eggs; this may be the damp soil beneath a rock, decomposing wood or leaf-litter. Some species from dry environments, such as the Galapagos land iguana, *Conolophus subcristatus*, dig deep holes in the sand until they reach a level where some moisture is retained. Where suitable egg-laying sites are scarce, there may be intense competition among females, and some eggs which have been laid may be disturbed by females coming along to lay later. In at least one observation, female iguanas also competed with a crocodile, *Crocodilus acutus*, for a nest site.

Occasionally, large caches of lizard eggs are found together in different stages of development. These obviously represent communal nest sites and are especially characteristic of many species of gecko. One of the largest recorded caches, however, belonged to the teiid lizard *Kentropyx calcaratus*, with a total of 800 eggs or remains of eggs. These were judged to have been laid by a number of females over a period of several years. There is no satisfactory explanation for the use of communal nest sites; they may simply be the result of a shortage of suitable places in which to lay.

Having deposited their eggs, most females then lose interest in them and subsequent development and hatching is left to chance, but females of some of the North American skinks belonging to the genus *Eumeces* (*E. fasciatus, obsoletus* and *laticeps*), and two anguids, (*Ophiosaurus ventralis* and *Gerrhonotus liocephalus*), coil around their eggs until they hatch, so guarding them from attack by small predators such as insects, and possibly 'incubating' them by warming their bodies in the sun and then returning to the clutch to transfer the heat. The skinks have even been known to move their eggs from one site to another by carrying them in their mouths, if conditions in the original site become unsuitable.

Females of live-bearing species, having nurtured their developing young throughout pregnancy, take no further interest in them after they are born. The young wriggle out of their enclosing membrane and are immediately independent. In some species, the females may eat the remains of their placentae, and one species, the night lizard, *Xantusia vigilis*, is thought to stimulate the young into moving by nudging them with her snout as she pulls off and eats their enclosing membranes. In other species, the young eat their own membranes – the only 'free' meal they will receive throughout their lives.

CLUTCH SIZE

The number of eggs laid per clutch (or young born) is partly dependent on the size of the species and the number of clutches laid each season. Thus, larger females lay larger clutches on average than small ones, both within species and between species, and species which lay only one clutch per year produce larger clutches than those which lay a number

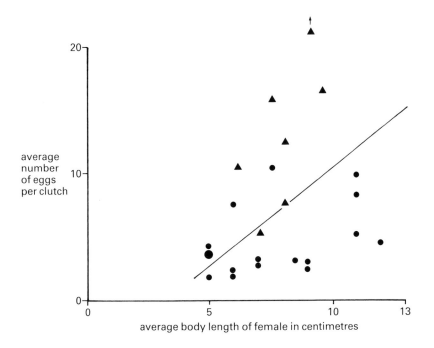

Fig. 13. Clutch size compared with body size for a selection of North American desert lizards. The line shows the average or 'expected' clutch size for any given body length in this sample – species above the line lay more eggs than would be expected and those below the line lay fewer. Note that six of the eleven species above the line are horned lizards (shown by triangles) and that only one horned lizard species is below the line.

of clutches. However, superimposed on this pattern are two others. First, in an evolutionary context, female lizards have the 'option' of laying either a lot of small eggs or a few large eggs. What they 'decide' to do will depend on many factors, including food supply and the predator situation. An example of this variation is found in the Australian skinks belonging to the genus *Tiliqua*. The blotched blue-tongued skink, *T. nigrolutea*, gives birth to five to ten large young, whereas the pink-tongued skink, *T. gerrardii*, produces 12–25 small young (with a record of 67), but the total weight of young, relative to the weight of the female, is similar.

The second complication concerns the taxonomic relationships of the lizards. In some families there is a tendency for all the members to produce a similar number of eggs or young. The geckos and snake lizards are the most obvious example of this situation; all species lay one or two eggs, or give birth to two young. This consistency is independent of size (save that those which lay one egg are all small), and the only variation in the respective species' output is in the size of the eggs and the number of clutches which they produce over a given period of time.

The most common clutch size in lizards is therefore two (due mainly to the approximately 700 species of geckos which lay this number). Clutches of one and three are also very frequent, but as the clutch size goes up, the number of species which average that size goes down.

A useful way of looking at the clutch size/egg size relationship is to divide the weight of the female by the weight of her clutch. This figure is known as the 'reproductive effort', i.e. it represents the amount of herself that the female puts into her offspring. This may vary from year to year according to the availability of food, etc., but most species of lizards have a reproductive effort of about 0.25 – their clutches weigh about one quarter of their body weight, although small species tend to have a higher reproductive effort than large ones (because they do not live as long and have to be as prolific as possible during their short lives). There are, however, some interesting exceptions: the horned lizards, *Phrynosoma*, of North America have higher reproductive efforts than would be expected from their size. A likely reason for this is that, being rounded in shape, they are not very good at running away from predators and rely mainly on camouflage instead (see Chapter 4). The extra load of a disproportionately large clutch of eggs is therefore not such a disadvantage to them as it would be to a species which needs to be agile.

GROWTH AND MATURITY

Generally, the mortality of lizards is at its highest during the first phase of their lives. Baby lizards are more vulnerable to predation because they are smaller (and therefore more species can eat them), because they are inexperienced at finding and catching food, and because they are not able to build up large food reserves. As they grow in size and experience, they gradually become less prone to predation, etc., and by the time some species, such as the large monitors and iguanas, are fully grown, they have virtually no predators and many undoubtedly die of 'old age'. However, at the other extreme, some of the smaller species, such as the side-blotched lizard, *Uta stansburiana*, are virtually annuals; they grow to maturity, breed and die all within one year. Of course, most lizards fall somewhere between these extremes and the 'average' life-span of most species, ignoring the high mortality of newly hatched or newborn babies, is probably somewhere around five to ten years.

TEMPERATURE-DEPENDENT SEX DETERMINATION (TSD)

One of the most interesting observations to come out of lizard research during the last ten years or so is the discovery that, in some species, the sex of the young depends on the temperature at which the eggs are incubated. For instance, in the case of the leopard gecko, *Eublepharus macularius*, a species which has been bred in enormous numbers by laboratories and private individuals, eggs which are kept at 28°C will result mostly in females whereas those kept at 32°C turn out to be males. Furthermore, it seems that there is a critical stage during incubation

Plate 50. A newly hatched day gecko leaves its eggshell. Its twin will hatch within the next day or so, and will probably be the same sex.

Plate 52. Parthenogenic lizards are found in several families, but it is especially prevalent in whiptails, such as *Cnemidophorus uniparens*, from the Arizona/Mexico border region.

are that every member of the population can breed and so they increase rapidly. In addition, females do not have to find a mate and if they wander into new territory they can go right ahead and begin to colonise it. The main disadvantage is that the offspring are identical to each other, and to their mother, i.e. they are clones, and the only way in which variation can occur is through chance mutation. This is fine for as long as conditions remain favourable, but if things begin to change, the species has little chance of adapting. So parthenogenic species obtain short-term advantages at the cost of long-term ones – they represent evolutionary dead-ends. Sexual reproduction, on the other hand, involves the combination of some genes from the mother with some from the father, leading to a huge number of permutations and variations. If conditions change, there is a much better chance that at least some of these variations would be in a position to cope with the new environment.

Chapter 7
Distribution
and Habitat

As an order, lizards occur almost everywhere except the polar regions, often by means of ingenious adaptations which enable them to survive adverse conditions, some of which have already been described in Chapters 2 and 3. The purpose of this chapter is first to get an overview of the global pattern of lizard distribution and then to focus down on the various kinds of habitats available to them and how these have been exploited. Finally, two very special habitats, deserts and oceanic islands, which are especially important to the study of lizard biology, are examined in detail.

PATTERNS OF DISTRIBUTION
The families of lizards can be broken down into three broad categories.

1. Families which have a more-or-less worldwide distribution – the geckos, the skinks and, to a lesser degree, the anguids.

2. Families which have a wide distribution in one particular large region of the world – the lacertids, agamids, iguanids, chameleons, teiids, cordylids and monitors.

3. Families which have a restricted distribution, or one in which relicts are scattered throughout the world – the night lizards, blind lizards, xenosaurs, heloderms and the Borneo earless monitor.

Widespread families may owe their success to one of two reasons: they may be ancient families which were present when the continents were joined together and were therefore able to spread around the globe without 'getting their feet wet', or they may contain species which are prone to rafting across expanses of ocean by clinging to vegetation and other debris which occasionally becomes detached from the land and is washed out to sea. (Because this event is more likely to take place in the hurricane belt, a region which lies almost entirely within the tropics, the chances of these islands being colonised are perhaps greater than we would imagine.) The present distribution of skinks and geckos probably reflects both of these factors; both groups are ancient, but both are also widely distributed on small volcanic islands and coral atolls which have never been part of a major landmass – the only way they could have arrived there is by rafting. In the case of the anguids, the fact that many species are legless burrowing forms indicates that they are probably less liable to accidental introduction by rafting and their distribution is probably due almost entirely to them having spread across the continents when they were joined (their absence in Australia, the earliest of the continents to break free, seems to confirm this).

The families with a more limited distribution are obviously successful, but seem to have blossomed after the land-masses on which they evolved had become isolated. Thus the iguanas are limited almost exclusively to the Americas, whereas their counterparts and close relatives, the agamids, are limited to the Old World, including Australia. Similarly, the teiids and the lacertids are equally restricted, to the New and Old Worlds respectively. The monitors seem to have their centre of distribution in South-East Asia, from where they have spread east into Africa and, especially, west into Australasia, where there has been a wide diversification of species. Two families have almost certainly arisen in Africa; the cordylids, which are still confined to the southern half of that continent, and the chameleons, which may have evolved in Madagascar (where the greatest number of species are found), and spread only as far as the Indian subcontinent and to extreme southern Europe and eastern Asia, where a single species lives.

The restricted families consist of 'oddities' – lizards which are well adapted to their own little niche but which, for some reason or another, have either become extinct elsewhere or have never spread. The night lizards are confined to a small area of North and Central America, the blind lizards (Dibamidae) and the Borneo earless monitor are found only in South-East Asia, mainly on islands, and the heloderms, although formerly more widespread, are found only in desert and semi-desert regions of North and Central America. The xenosaurs, if indeed they constitute a valid family, are found in limited localities in Central America and southern China, which would lead to the conclusion that the family was formerly far more widespread but has contracted drastically due to extinctions. An equivalent situation is found in the eublepharine (or eublepharid) geckos, with small groups of species in North and Central America, Africa, the Middle East, South-East Asia and Japan, all completely isolated from each other by thousands of miles.

Looking at the main zoogeographical regions of the world (Fig. 14) in turn, it is interesting to compare the relative richness of each:

1. In the Neoarctic region there are eight families, two of which, the heloderms and the night lizards, are endemic. Small to medium-sized iguanids are numerous and exist in a variety of forms and habitats, and the anguids are also well represented. The whiptail family consists of several species of the genus *Cnemidophorus* which appear to be undergoing fairly rapid evolution at present, and the skinks are represented mainly by members of the genus *Eumeces*. The number of gecko species is relatively small, and three of the four species of xenosaurs are present. Amphisbaenians are present; there is a single species in Florida and all three species of the strange genus *Bipes* in Mexico.

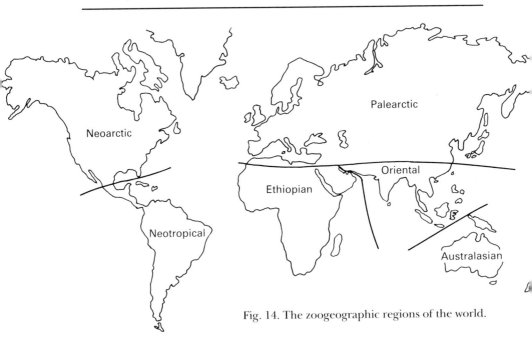

Fig. 14. The zoogeographic regions of the world.

2. In the Neotropical region there are five families, but none are endemic. The most important family is that of the iguanids, but there are also many micro- and macro-teiids, a selection of skinks and anguids and numerous small geckos, the most characteristic of which are the small sphaerodactylines. Amphisbaenians are also found here, notably the large species belonging to the genus *Amphisbaena.*

3. In the Palaearctic region there are six families. The most prominent of these is that of the wall lizards and their relatives (Lacertidae) in Europe, and the agamas in Asia, but there are also small numbers of skinks, geckos and anguids as well as a single species of chameleon. A solitary species of amphisbaenian is found in Europe, and several others occur in Asia.

4. In the Ethiopean region there are seven families, one of which, the girdled lizards, is endemic. There are large numbers of agamas, skinks, geckos, chameleons and lacertids and two species of monitors, while four species of iguanas live on Madagascar. There are many species of amphisbaenians in the Middle East as well as in continental Africa, occupying a variety of habitats.

5. In the Oriental region there is a total of ten families, including two small families, the Dibamidae and the Lanthanotidae, which are endemic. There is a large number of agamas, especially arboreal species, many geckos, lacertids and skinks, several anguids and monitors, one of the four species of xenosaurs and one chameleon. The amphisbaenians are also present in small numbers.

6. The Australasian region has the least number of families represented – four – but all of these show a remarkable degree of diversification. All four families, the geckos, agamas, skinks and monitors, contain a variety of forms which have adapted to a wide range of habitats. There are no amphisbaenians in Australasia.

HABITATS

Each region of the world has a suite of habitats, made up basically of the effects of climate on the underlying geology and topography. Often, broad categories of habitat types are common to two or more regions, e.g. deserts, mountains, etc., but each may also differ in some subtle way from place to place. Thus, the deserts of North America, Africa, Asia and Australia differ from each other, even though they have similar climatic conditions, and although these differences may be slight, they are important factors in determining how many species are able to survive there and how they go about making a living. Conversely, similar habitats often create similar difficulties for their inhabitants, and the adaptations which allow one species to live in, say, a North American desert, are often mirrored in unrelated species from other deserts.

Lizards could loosely be divided into 'specialists' and 'generalists'. The specialists are those species which have committed themselves to one particular habitat and life-style and modified their shape and behaviour in such a way that they can exploit this to the full. An example of this is the granite night lizard, *Xantusia henshawi*. This species lives only in the narrow crevices formed by exfoliating rock; its body is greatly flattened from top to bottom and its activity-pattern is entirely nocturnal because this habitat tends to occur in regions where extremes of heat cause the rocks to flake. In southern Africa, the flat lizards, *Platysaurus*, have evolved in parallel because similar conditions prevail, although in this case the lizards are active during the day. None of these lizards is ever found in a habitat other than its own specialised little niche, but they are so well adapted that they face little competition from other species. Chameleons, horned lizards and amphisbaenians are other groups of species which have undergone extreme modification in order to claim a habitat for themselves.

On the other hand, many species of lizards are not restricted to a single niche and may be found thriving under a variety of conditions. These species include the wall lizards, genus *Podarcis*, of Europe and the whiptails, *Cnemidophorus*, from North America. These and other species are what we think of as 'typical' lizards – cylindrical, with four legs and a long tapering tail. They seem equally at home whether running across open terrain or climbing on rocks or in bushes, and may even resort to swimming if necessary. They are opportunistic, and are able to move rapidly into newly created habitats.

Each community of lizards is made up of some specialists and some generalists, and the ways in which they interact are of great interest to community ecologists, telling us much about the way evolution works.

Although a comprehensive survey is not possible here, it is useful to discuss briefly some of the more obvious habitats and generalise about the types of lizards which could be expected to live there.

Aquatic habitats have not proven to be appealing to many lizards. The only truly aquatic species is the marine iguana, *Amblyrhynchus cristatus*, from the Galapagos, which possesses salt glands, a flattened, rudder-like tail and certain physiological capabilities associated with its life-style. Other species that are associated with water include the Chinese crocodile lizard, the European Schreiber's lizard, the water dragons, *Physignathus*, from southern Asia and Australia, a few of the large iguanids such as the basilisks, the teiid *Dracaena* from South America, half a dozen species of monitor and several skinks. None of these species, however, has any notable adaptations for an aquatic life-style, except the monitors, which have flattened tails and nostrils situated towards the top of their snouts.

Forests in temperate regions are usually poor in lizard species – the perpetual shade, coupled to a cool climate, makes the maintenance of a suitable body temperature difficult – but in the tropics rain forests are the home of a number of arboreal, terrestrial and burrowing species. The arboreal species in particular are often modified in some way which helps them to live in the trees; obvious examples are the 'wings' of the flying dragons, *Draco*, and the flying geckos, *Ptychozoon*, but long claws or expanded toe-pads for climbing, and a prehensile tail are also quite commonly seen. A few species, notably the chameleons, have their digits rearranged into a specialised grasping organ, and many arboreal species are green. Because opportunities for basking are limited, many forest species are thermal conformers (see page 43).

Grasslands and savanna (and, in recent times, agricultural regions) may contain a good selection of species, although mostly of the more generalised form with few adaptations. Many have long powerful hind legs and a long tail and these alert species tend to rely on rapid locomotion in order to escape from predators. Several species hide in holes in the ground, either those of rodents or self-constructed, whereas others make use of piles of rocks, dry stone walls, etc.

Rocks and outcrops are often very rich in lizard species, especially in the warmer parts of the world. They provide plenty of good refuges, from the heat and cold as well as from predators, and are often rich in insects and other food. The flattened shape of some species has already been mentioned; other adaptations include long claws and toe-pads for climbing and coloration which blends with the particular rock on which they are living. Species which use crevices or holes in which to hide may have well-armoured, spiny tails, and some have a habit of inflating their bodies with air in order to wedge themselves firmly into their retreats.

A large number of lizards, and all amphisbaenians, live beneath the ground, either in the upper layers of leaf-litter or in tunnel systems in the soil. These burrowing species are often recognisable by their elongated cylindrical bodies, shiny scales and pointed snouts. These species are obliged to become thermal conformers, although they may indulge in limited 'basking' by coming close to the surface where the substrate is warm.

High mountain ranges provide limited habitats for lizards because they suffer the disadvantage of low temperatures, especially at night. A small number of species, however, is found at high altitude, especially in the Andes where members of the genera *Liolaemus* and *Centrura* are commonly found up to 3,000 m (9,800 ft) and extend even higher in places. Like species in other cold environments, most of these species give birth to living young, and many are dark in colour.

LIZARDS IN DESERTS

Lizard communities in deserts deserve special mention because of the extent to which they have exploited this habitat – probably more than any other vertebrate group. Every desert region has its own characteristic community of lizards, over half of all lizard families being represented in this type of habitat. These widely unrelated species, living in completely separate parts of the world, have all had similar problems to solve – it should not be surprising, then, that many of them have evolved along similar lines, both as regards their appearance and their habits.

The reason why lizards have been so successful at colonising deserts hinges upon the fact that they are ectotherms. In the first place, deserts tend to be hot, and therefore the problem of maintaining an adequate body temperature for at least some part of the day requires little effort on the part of the lizard – just being there is sufficient. Allied to this are their low energy requirements. Endothermic animals, such as birds and mammals, use a large portion of their food intake to maintain their body temperatures. Since lizards do not need to 'spend' their energy in this way they are able to exist on a much lower budget – it has been estimated that a small lizard can survive for a month on the same amount of food as a small bird requires for a single day. Since deserts generally provide only a limited food supply, any animal which can manage on less is at an advantage.

If we look at a community of lizards in a desert region, it is possible to see how the member species are divided up into a number of categories: size, activity pattern, food preferences and so on. There is little or no overlap among the species, and they seem to have shared out the resources in the most efficient way possible. More important, it is usually possible to find that in any two or more deserts, each niche will be filled by a similar species, unrelated, but having many characteristics in common. Thus, in the deserts of the American south-west, the horned lizards, *Phrynosoma*, bear a striking resemblance to the Australian thorny devil, *Moloch horridus*. Both have carved out a niche for themselves (specialising in a diet of ants) which has moulded them into virtual replicas despite their separate ancestries.

Similarly, there are herbivorous species in most deserts, small insectivores, and species which prey on smaller lizards. Naturally, food is

Plate 53. Lizards are more at home in deserts than any other vertebrate group. Even this harsh landscape in Baja California provides niches for a number of specialised species of xantusiids, iguanids, teiids and geckos.

only one parameter, or dimension, of a species' niche and others can be equally important. In this way, there are nocturnal and diurnal species in each community, terrestrial and semi-arboreal species, and species which spend a large part of their lives beneath the surface of the sand or soil.

LIZARDS ON ISLANDS

Whereas the study of desert lizards is teaching us a lot about the way in which *communities* of animals develop and interact, studies of lizards on islands can teach us about the way in which *species* evolve, just as the finches of the Galapagos islands gave inspiration to Charles Darwin in the nineteenth century. At the same time, they provide important clues about the history of the earth and the way in which the land-masses were formed and moved about.

Because lizards are unable, by and large, to cross wide expanses of ocean, the colonisation of islands is an infrequent occurrence (compared, for example, with the rate at which birds colonise islands). Therefore, once a species becomes isolated it is often left to evolve independently of its parent stock for many millions of years. New species often arise in this way, shaped to their new environment, and so each island or group of islands becomes a natural experiment, a kind of living museum in which the exhibits hold clues to our understanding of important biological concepts.

The most familiar and studied group of island lizards are those of the West Indies: dozens of species of *Anolis* are found throughout the region – large islands have several species, small ones have fewer, often only a

which distinguish them from their ancestors, but since the process has had less time to act on them, the differences are less pronounced.

Another aspect to island zoogeography is that because the animals which do manage to colonise them belong to a fairly exclusive club, they are able to diversify into niches which are already taken on the mainland by competing species (not just lizards). In other words, if only one or two lizards reach a certain island, they have the habitat to themselves and can exploit it more fully than if there were many species using the same resources. Under certain conditions, this can lead to very high population densities; a thorough study of the skinks of Cousin Island, in the Seychelles group, showed that two species of skink, *Mabuya sechellensis* and *M. wrightii*, existed in densities of 1,393 and 320 lizards per hectare respectively. Because *M. wrightii* is much the larger of the two, their total biomass was similar (44 and 73 kg/90 and 161 lb per hectare). This enormous mass of lizards is supported by seabird colonies for which the island is famous; the lizards scavenge around nests and feed on bird faeces, fish dropped by the birds and broken eggs. Although this food is seasonal, it is so rich and abundant that the lizards are able to rely on the fat stored during the birds' breeding season. They owe their success to the fact that they are able to make use of a resource for which there are no other takers.

Similarly, the Komodo dragon, *Varanus komodoensis*, the world's largest lizard, lives on a group of small islands forming part of the Indonesian archipelago. The dragon is probably able to grow to such a great size because there are no other large carnivorous mammals living on the island, leaving a vacant niche which the lizards were able to exploit.

The study of lizards living on islands can thus help us to understand several important aspects of general biology: speciation by isolation, the way in which animals move around the world, and the results of competitive release. In addition, their distribution can often help to crystallise ideas about the geological history of the world and the events which have shaped it.

Finally, as we have seen elsewhere, the study of lizards living on islands also demonstrates just how vulnerable these communities and their member species are – it would be a great tragedy if these animals, which have taught us so much about our origins, and still have much to teach us, are allowed to join the ranks of the extinct reptiles.

Chapter 8
Lizards in Captivity

Serious study of lizards often involves the maintenance of a few specimens in captivity. In addition, their bright colours and harmless nature have ensured that they have always been popular among the more adventurous 'pet-keepers'. In the past, a poor understanding of their biology, especially in connection with their dietary and thermal requirements, and their social behaviour, has led to them being kept in unsatisfactory conditions and eventually to the untimely death of most captive specimens, even in the hands of experienced herpetologists.

Even now, some groups of species are still not easily kept alive, much less persuaded to breed in captivity, but the situation is improving. Unfortunately, requirements vary greatly from species to species and so it is only possible to give the most generalised instructions here. Additional information can often be deduced from intelligent interpretation of accounts of each species' distribution and ecology, as given in this book and elsewhere. In addition, there is a specialised but growing literature on the care of reptiles and amphibians in captivity and access to this is often best achieved through membership of one of the herpetological societies.

Most failures are due to a poor initial choice of species. It is important not to patronise the trade in those animals which are difficult to keep alive as this only encourages collectors and dealers to continue to trade in these species. If possible, try to obtain captive-bred juveniles, although these are only available for a limited number of species. Failing this, choose small common species rather than large spectacular lizards such as green iguanas, tegus, monitors and chameleons, etc., which are very difficult to care for and will almost certainly die quickly in the hands of the novice. Success with less demanding species will be satisfying and educational, and the experience so gained will be useful if more difficult species are to be attempted later.

ACCOMMODATION

Lizards require varying amounts of space, depending not only on their size but also on their activity patterns. Whereas a small gecko may live indefinitely in a plastic box, a large monitor or iguanid would require an entire house to even begin to approach its ideal space requirements. Choice of species is therefore of the greatest importance and, in general, small lizards such as geckos or skinks are the easiest to care for. In addition, it is always preferable to aim to accommodate a group of small animals in a given space rather than a solitary large one – not only will there then be a chance that they will breed, but it will be possible to witness some of the social interactions which make lizard-keeping so interesting.

Small lizards can be kept in a cage in which a simulation of their natural biotope is created; they often stay in better health if they are given the opportunity to behave just as they would in the wild. Thus, rock-dwelling species can be given a pile of rocks in which to hide and forage, and arboreal species can be given a tall cage furnished with some dead branches and one or two living plants (preferably in pots for easy replacement). Burrowing species can be given artificial burrows in the form of clay pipes incorporated into the substrate, or their cage may have a false floor with an entrance leading to a lower portion.

Animals which must be kept in isolation because they are young, sick, about to lay eggs, etc., can be kept more simply and hygienically in small plastic boxes, but it is still important to provide security in the form of something to hide under, and a substrate on which the lizard can gain a good purchase. The horticultural clay beads sold for use on greenhouse staging have proven to be an ideal artificial substrate, but gravel or sand may also be employed.

HEATING

All lizards require heat, but each species varies in its precise requirement. In addition, individuals require different amounts of heat at different times of the day and year. The best arrangement is to give them a choice by setting up a thermal gradient in their cage. This is achieved by applying the heat locally at one end. Two types of heat are possible: radiant heat in the form of a spotlight, or bottom heat in the form of a heat-pad or cable laid under the cage. Species which habitually bask obviously require a source of radiant heat, but it may still be necessary to supplement this with bottom heat in order to maintain a suitable background temperature, especially at night when the basking light should be turned off. Males of basking species are often highly territorial; if more than one is to be kept in a cage, not only should this be large enough to accommodate more than one territory, but a basking light should be provided for each territory.

It is difficult to give guidelines for temperature requirements due to the variation noted above, but a gradient starting at 20°C and rising to 35°C should suit most species, although a few desert lizards require an even higher temperature (up to 40°C) immediately beneath the heat-source. Lizards which are continually trying to get closer to the heat source and which are not feeding vigorously are probably being kept too cool.

LIGHTING

Lizards which bask, and this includes most species to some extent, require sunlight, or an artificial equivalent, in order to synthesise Vitamin D3. Without this they are unable to mobilise the calcium and phosphorus in their diet, with the end result that their bones are not properly formed. Lights which give out increased amounts of ultra-violet wavelengths are available, and these appear to be a suitable substitute for sunlight. They should be lit whenever the basking light is on, so that the lizard obtains its 'dose' of ultra-violet at the same time as it is raising its body temperature (as in the wild). Note that these lights have a limited life, after which the U-V output diminishes, and they should be replaced according to the data supplied with them.

DIET

The diet of the lizard obviously depends on its natural food, although most insectivorous species can be persuaded to accept readily available food – animals such as crickets, locusts, mealworms and waxworms. A good variety should be given, and commercially available insects should be supplemented whenever possible with small invertebrates caught in the garden (no insecticides, please). Some of the larger species can be given dead rodents or chicks, although these may have to be moved about in front of their noses before they are recognised as food. Herbivorous lizards can be fed leaf vegetables and fruit (chopped or grated for juveniles) and they may also take small quantities of insects when available. Some of the more omnivorous species will happily accept canned dog and cat food, which makes life easy, since these products are often reinforced with vitamins and minerals.

Whatever diet is used, it is a good idea to sprinkle it with one of the commercially available reptile supplements. These contain essential elements which are often lacking in captive diets, and should be used on every feed. Females which are kept for breeding will benefit from extra calcium and phosphorus, which can be obtained in the form of tablets sold for lactating dogs, ground cuttlefish bone or crushed eggshells.

Although the amount of food required varies, many species eat enormous quantities, especially while they are still growing. Insufficient food is often the cause of failure to breed or low resistance to disease; most lizards should be allowed to eat all that they want to, and it is only necessary to withold or ration food in the case of large animals which are unlikely to obtain enough exercise in captivity and therefore become obese.

In general, herbivorous lizards require more food than insectivorous ones, and feeding of these species should take place every day. Otherwise, food can be offered every two days, giving the lizards time and the incentive to root out crickets, etc., which have crawled beneath rocks and so on – this will encourage the lizards to forage, as well as preventing a feral population of crickets, which can wreak havoc among plants.

BREEDING

Breeding will take place only when environmental conditions are right – this is as good a reason as any for breeding the lizards since it indicates that they are being kept properly. The lizards must be well fed, have the correct type of cage, a suitable temperature and a light source. Obviously, there must also be at least one member of each sex present. This can often be established by the presence of dorsal crests, etc., or pre-anal and femoral pores in adult males (see page 27). Note that the sexes of some species, especially skinks, are not easily told apart and it may be necessary to obtain a group of, say, four individuals and study their behaviour towards one another in order to establish one or more pairs – mature males display to each other frequently and may fight.

Most species are stimulated to breed by one or more environmental triggers: longer days, higher temperatures, higher humidity, etc. It may be necessary to investigate the habits of the species concerned more closely, or they may simply cue into the prevailing conditions under which they are kept. It is usually best to isolate females which are carrying eggs or young, which should be obvious from their increasing girth. They should be given an identical or similar cage to that which they are used to and, in the case of oviparous species, a suitable site for the eggs to be laid. Geckos, which lay calcareous eggs, will often stick these to the sides of the cage or to the underside of a piece of bark, inside a bamboo tube, etc. These eggs can be left in place or moved to a smaller cage to incubate. Other egg-laying species must have an area of damp substrate, such as sand, peat or a mixture of the two, in which to burrow and lay. Their eggs have permeable shells and soon dry out if not provided with moisture. After they have been laid, they should be transferred to a small plastic box, complete with the damp substrate, and kept in a warm place until they hatch. The best incubation temperature is usually about 28°C, but varies slightly from species to species. Note carefully the section on temperature dependent sex determination (Chapter 6) – failure to do so may result in young which are all the same sex!

Young lizards will require separate accommodation from the adults, otherwise they will, at best, be beaten to the food or, at worst, eaten. Sometimes it is necessary to rear each youngster in isolation in order to avoid fighting and competition for food.

SUMMARY

Keeping lizards can be a good way of learning about them and their habits. It can also be a satisfying hobby in its own right. However, they are not as easy to care for as most domestic animals and often require special attention which can only be given if their biology is properly understood. The information given above consists of the most basic guidelines, and is intended only as a starting point. The titles of a small number of books and journals which deal with the most commonly available species are included in the bibliography. As there is at present no detailed manual for the keeping of every species which may be available, contact with experienced persons, through membership of one of the specialist societies, is strongly advised.

Chapter 9

The Classification
of Lizards

As with all classes of animals, the lizard species are grouped together into units, the object of which is to simplify their study. These units are, in descending order of hierarchy, families, genera and species. Intermediate groupings, consisting of sub-families, sub-genera and sub-species are also used occasionally. None of these grouping are (at least they should not be) arbitrarily assigned, but should reflect the degree to which each animal is related to others. Relatedness, in turn, is a consequence of evolution; if a species broke away from its ancestors millions of years ago, it will not be as closely related to that stock as one which broke away only a few thousand years ago. Unfortunately, we have no way of knowing precisely how long each population of lizards has been isolated from its parent stock and so the degree of relatedness must be assessed on anatomical or physiological similarities and differences. This method is based on the assumption that mutations occur at a fairly constant rate, and that the longer the time which has elapsed, the greater the number of mutations and therefore the greater the cumulative differences.

It has been stressed in several parts of this book that one of the most fascinating aspects of lizard biology has been convergent evolution – species which live under similar conditions often come to look and act like each other even though they are not closely related and are geographically widely separated. This can obviously cause confusion when assigning lizards to a certain species, genera or family, and former methods of classification, which relied heavily on an animal's appearance, were often misleading. If classification is to be useful, it is necessary to ignore these superficial similarities and attempt to deduce the ancestry and relatedness of the various forms.

There are now many tools and techniques which enable taxonomists to do just this, but not all species have been thoroughly studied. In addition, there is often resistance to the splitting or combining of groupings which have remained stable for several decades. Finally, because the concepts of species, genera and families are 'unnatural', i.e. they have been invented by biologists as a convenient means of studying plants and animals and communicating information, there will always be personal differences of opinion over whether certain animals are distinct enough to be called species, or whether they belong in this family or that.

All this can cause problems for non-taxonomists when names change for no apparent reason, or animals are moved from one family to another. The taxonomy of lizards is especially problematical at the present time because large-scale revisions are underway and the situation is somewhat chaotic. As the remainder of this chapter is devoted to accounts of 17 recognised families of lizards, readers should be aware that the groupings used are not carved in stone, but that they represent a fairly accurate overview of current thinking.

The most important revision in recent years concerns the groupings of the most primitive species of lizards, the snake-lizards and the geckos. Although I have retained the 'traditional' classification in the main text, readers should be aware that Kluge, in a paper published in 1987, has proposed a major rearrangement, details of which are given below.

This classification involves four main changes:

1. The eublepharine geckos are moved from the Gekkonidae to a separate family, the Eublepharidae.

2. The sub-family Diplodactylinae is moved from the Gekkonidae to the Pygopodidae.

3. The genus *Teratoscincus* is moved from the Gekkoninae to a separate sub-family, the Teratoscincinae.

4. The sphaerodactyline geckos are no longer regarded as belonging to a separate sub-family but are combined with the Gekkoninae.

ARRANGEMENT USED IN THIS BOOK , BASED ON KLUGE (1967)

Family Pygopodidae (snake-lizards)
   (no sub-families)
Family Gekkonidae
  Sub-family Eublepharinae (eublepharine geckos)
  Sub-family Diplodactylinae (diplodactyline geckos)
  Sub-family Gekkoninae (typical geckos)
  Sub-family Sphaerodactylinae (sphaerodactyline geckos)

NEW ARRANGEMENT, PROPOSED BY KLUGE (1987)

Family Eublepharidae
   (no sub-families)
Family Gekkonidae
  Sub-family Gekkoninae (typical geckos)
  Sub-family Teratoscincinae (teratoscincine geckos)
Family Pygopodidae
  Sub-family Diplodactylinae
  Sub-family Pygopodinae (snake-lizards)

GEKKONIDAE – Geckos (see note on page 105)

NUMBER OF SPECIES: Approximately 830

DISTRIBUTION
Throughout the tropical and sub-tropical world, including hundreds of oceanic islands.

Geckos are among the most primitive of lizards, but also among the most successful. The 800 or so species are found in almost every tropical and sub-tropical region, as well as in several more temperate ones. These are the lizards which are best known to visitors to the tropics and sub-tropics, many of them being closely associated with human activities. In fact, it is not usually necessary to go out looking for geckos – they make house-calls, and are the ultimate lounge-lizards. They are as much a part of the tropics as the slowly turning ceiling fans, as they wage an unceasing war against the less lovable of our commensals, mopping up the flies, mosquitoes and cockroaches which accompany us wherever we go. As pest controllers, they have a formidable armoury; their ability to adhere to smooth surfaces, including glass, puts them on an equal 'footing' with their prey, while their stealth and speed offers little chance to a reckless cockroach. For a herpetologist, there are few pleasures to compare with eating a well-earned evening meal in exotic surroundings while watching the local gecko population systematically eliminating potential bedmates!

Plate 57. A house gecko of indeterminate species, resting upside down on the ceiling of a hotel bedroom in Sumatra. A pair of large, fully developed eggs can clearly be seen in the abdomen of this female.

Plate 59. *Coleonyx variegatus* is one of several eublepharid geckos from North and Central America. It is a nocturnal desert species which feeds on small insects. Note the functional eyelids, absent in most other geckos.

gecko. *Holodactylus* is the other West African genus, with two species found in the Ethiopian region.

The North American contingent of the sub-family all belong to the genus *Coleonyx*; they are collectively known as banded geckos. In these species, males are easily recognised due to the presence of a pair of small thorn-like spurs which grow from the base of the tail. Seven species range from the deserts of the southern United States down into Panama. The most common species is *C. variegatus* of south-western North America. It grows to about 7.5 cm (3 in) from snout to vent, and about twice this in total length. This species has small granular scales and the bands, which are most prominent in juveniles, are of brown and

kos were living and emerges into the desert at

since recent proposals are concerned mainly

they are dealt with separately.

C. brevis is the Texas banded gecko, which inhabits the arid region which straddles the border between Mexico and southern Texas. In habits and appearance it is rather similar to *C. variegatus*, but its banded pattern breaks down into numerous small spots as it becomes adult. This species also has smooth, silky skin, while the remaining species all have a tougher, tuberculate skin, rather like that of the *Eublepharus* species mentioned above.

From the same region as *C. brevis*, but with a more limited range, *C. reticulatus* is much rarer and grows slightly larger. It is said to use its tail as an aid in climbing. The most enigmatic species of all is probably *C. switaki*, the barefoot gecko. This species was only described in 1974, despite living in the desert foothills of southern California and adjacent Baja California, an area with a superabundance of both amateur and professional herpetologists. It has obviously escaped notice for so long because it has secretive habits, living among boulders and exfoliated rocks and rarely venturing out onto open ground, even at night. Its sporadic appearances have earned it the local name of 'magic gecko'.

The remaining three species are predominantly Central American in distribution. *C. fasciatus* has been found in scattered localities in western Mexico, but its habits are little known, only a handful having been discovered. *C. elegans* is a far more common species, especially in the Yucatan region of Mexico, although it also ranges north into Vera Cruz and Oaxaca and south into northern Guatemala. This is the largest species of banded gecko, reaching a maximum size of almost 10 cm (4 in). There is a tendency in this species for some individuals to develop longitudinal stripes rather than bands. *C. mitratus* is the most southerly species and lives in the humid regions of Central America, from southern Guatemala to northern Panama. Little is known of its natural history.

Eublepharine geckos are represented in the Far East by two genera. Two species of *Goniurosaurus* are known: *G. kuroiwae*, from a number of Japanese islands, and *G. lichtenfelderi*, from islands in the Gulf of Tonkin and Hainan, China (these were formerly placed in the genus *Eublepharus*). The remaining genus is *Aleuroscalabotes*, containing a single species, *A. felinus*, in Malaysia, Sumatra and Borneo. This gecko is distinct from the rest of the eublepharines in being elongated and arboreal. It lives in rain forest habitats and is sometimes known as the cat gecko.

SPHAERODACTYLINAE

The members of this sub-family are all found in the New World, with their distribution centred on the Caribbean region. All are small, with toe-pads absent or poorly developed, and all lay a single, hard-shelled calcareous egg. Most of them are diurnal, some are brightly coloured, and they have no voices. There are 120 species in five genera.

The two predominant genera are *Sphaerodactylus* and *Gonatodes*. Three species of *Sphaerodactylus* occur in Florida, although at least two of them have been introduced from the West Indies. The ashy gecko, *S. cinereus*, is typical of the genus. It grows to a maximum size of 7.5 cm (3 in), and is

Plate 60. The ashy gecko, *Sphaerodactylus cinereus*, from Florida. This specimen, full grown at about 7 cm (2.5 in), is in the process of shedding its skin.

brown with a dense covering of lighter coloured spots over the whole of its body (Plate 60). The young are completely different, being boldly marked with dark crossbands and having a red tail. Some 60 species are found among the West Indian islands, many of them living on Cuba and Hispaniola, and others are found in Central America.

Gonatodes species tend to be slightly larger, and many are brightly coloured, especially the males which are often completely different in appearance from the females (Plate 46). In Florida there is one species, *Gonatodes albogularis*, the yellow-headed gecko, again introduced. In this species the male has a yellow or ochre head and a dark blue or black body. Females and juveniles are mottled brown. The natural range of this species is very large and includes Central America and northern South America as well as Cuba, Hispaniola and Jamaica. Several species of *Gonatodes* are found on the islands of Trinidad and Tobago, including *G. vittatus*, in which the male has a broad mid-dorsal stripe of white, bordered by black, and *G. ceciliae*, in which the almost black male is decorated with a deep red blotch on each shoulder.

Other species of *Gonatodes* extend well into South America, as do the remaining genera, *Pristurus Pseudogonatodes, Coleodactylus* and *Lepidoblepharis*. All of these species are active during the day, although they are not conspicuous lizards and move about quietly in the shade. Several of them can be found around houses, where they make good use of the cover provided by timber and other human debris, and by of

GEKKONINAE

This is by far the largest and most widely distributed sub-family, containing 607 species in 63 genera, and it is only possible here to mention some of the more distinctive species.

The archetypal gecko is the tokay, *Gekko gecko*, a large species from South-East Asia. Their harsh 'to-kay' vocalisation is produced loudly and raucously. They are nearly always found in or around houses, where each individual makes its home in a crevice or cavity which becomes its permanent retreat and which is vigorously defended against trespassers. Even human intruders are confronted by an aggressive display involving a gaping mouth, which is often followed up by a real attack in which the powerful jaws clamp shut over the nearest finger, causing some discomfort! In colour, the tokay is rather flamboyant for a gecko, its body being bluish-grey, covered with an even sprinkling of orange spots. Several other members of the genus are found in South-East Asia (Plate 57), mostly large, and with similar habits, although none are as common or as brightly coloured as the tokay.

Hemidactylus is a large genus, all members of which have well-developed toe-pads. Members of this genus are especially well suited for accidental transportation, and some, for instance *H. turcicus* and *H. frenatus*, are found in so many far-flung places that it can be difficult to establish their true origins. Typically, they are medium-sized lizards, brown to pinkish in colour, with a scattering of tubercular scales among their granular ones. Apart from houses, they live in a variety of habitats, including rocks, dry-stone walls and trees. The other great traveller in the family is *Gehyra mutilata*, which is found on many of the oceanic islands of the Pacific region as well as in Thailand, Indo-China and Sri Lanka.

Staying in Asia, the genus *Ptychozoon* has already been mentioned in connection with its aeronautical tendencies (see page 21). At least two species are found on the Malayan peninsula and in Thailand, and a third comes from the Philippines, but they are all similar to one another. They live most of their lives on tree-trunks, such as those of coconut palms, and glide to the ground or to lower perches if pursued. Also in this region is a large number of naked-toed geckos, belonging to the genus *Gymnodactylus*. These are predominantly ground or rock-dwelling species, although they may climb into low bushes or up onto the trunks of trees. Some are marked with crossbars or spots, and several have banded tails. These are the most distinctive genera found in South and South-Eastern Asia, although the region is swarming with a variety of other small, brownish geckos with similar habits.

Western Asia and the Middle East have a fairly distinctive gecko fauna, including several desert-adapted kinds as well as the more typical climbing species. Notable among them are *Teratoscincus scincus*, a ground-dwelling species from Iran and adjacent regions, where it occurs at an altitude of up to 1,830 m (6,000 ft), and the Arabian peninsula. This species is peculiar in its defence behaviour; if approached it slowly waves its tail from side to side, causing a row of modified scales to rub

Plate 67. *Rhacodactylus chahoua*, a large diplodactyline gecko from New Caledonia.

Plate 68. *Diplodactylus taenicauda*, the golden-tailed gecko from Australia. This species squirts threads of mucus from glands in its tail if it is threatened.

built species with an unusual pattern of green, brown and pinkish mottling over its back and tail. This makes for good camouflage when it is at rest on a lichen-covered tree-trunk (Plate 67).

The natural history of these and other diplodactyline geckos from New Caledonia and neighbouring islands is not well known, but a large number of species are found in Australia and, although some are very rare, they have, on the whole, been better studied. Among the strangest are the six species known as knob-tailed geckos, belonging to the genus *Nephrurus*. These species all live in arid habitats, have large heads, spindly legs and short tails which end in a knob (Plate 6).

The largest genus, however, is *Diplodactylus*, with over 20 species. They have slightly dilated tips to their digits, and include arboreal as well as terrestrial species. They are a varied group of lizards, in which the tail is often modified, sometimes to carry a double row of spines, as in *D. ciliaris* (Plate 9), but more often as a fat storage organ, as in *D. elderi*. In both these species, as well as in several others, the tail also contains glands which exude a noxious substance if the lizard is molested. Yet another species, *D. conspicillatus*, has a thick bony tail which it uses to plug the abandoned burrows of spiders, where the geckos hide, head downwards, during the day (see page 64).

Many *Diplodactylus* species are quite brightly coloured; for instance, the golden-tailed gecko, *D. taenicauda*, in which the body is reticulated with black and grey, while a bright orange stripe runs along the top of the tail and onto part of the body (Plate 68). The large eyes are also orange in colour. This species is arboreal, and the tail is glandular (which may account for its bright warning colour).

The genus *Oedura* contains nine species, which are known collectively as velvet geckos. At one time they were thought to be more closely related to the eublepharines than to the diplodactyline geckos. However, they do have toe-pads and are mostly arboreal, although some species live among rocks. All are secretive, the arboreal species usually resting behind peeling bark during the day and the rock-dwelling species wedging themselves into crevices under flaking rock, etc. For this reason, several of them are greatly flattened, to enable them to crawl into the narrow spaces between bark and tree-trunk (e.g. *O. monilis*), or behind flaking rock (e.g. *O. coggeri*). Individuals of *O. castelnaui* will use either type of habitat, depending on which part of their range they live in. All species of *Oedura* are highly drought-adapted, and can survive many months without food or water.

Phyllurus species are known as leaf-tailed geckos. They are bizarre in appearance due to the spiny tubercles which cover their heads, bodies, limbs and tails. Three of the four species have greatly flattened, leaf-shaped tails; the fourth, *P. caudiannulatus*, has a straightforward tapering tail. *P. cornutus* (Plate 38) is a large arboreal species growing to over 20 cm (8 in) in total length. The similar *P. salebrosus* may also be found on

PYGOPODIDAE – Snake Lizards (see note on page 105)

NUMBER OF SPECIES: 31

DISTRIBUTION

The snake lizards are confined to Australia and a few neighbouring islands, including New Britain and New Guinea.

All of the snake lizards are without limbs, although they retain the vestiges of their hind limbs in the form of small scaly flaps at each side of the cloaca (and are sometimes known as flap-footed lizards or scaly-footed lizards for this reason). In some species they are used occasionally to aid locomotion and for display. The eyes are covered by a transparent scale, the brille or spectacle, as in geckos and snakes, and they use their tongue to wipe away sand and dirt. Their tails are readily discarded. As far as is known, all species lay two soft-shelled eggs per clutch, and communication is by vocalisation, despite the fact that they have no external ear-openings. Like the geckos, they have a pair of small spur-like bones at the base of the tail, and there are several other important characteristics, in addition to those listed, which link the snake lizards to the geckos, and so the two families are thought to be very closely related.

Their elongated form is probably an adaptation to burrowing, and some species are 'sand-swimmers', but typically they emerge onto the surface, usually at night, in order to feed.

Eight genera are recognised, of which four have only one species each. The largest genus is *Delma*, with 13 species. All its members are about 30 cm (12 in) in length, with the tail comprising about one-quarter of this total. These medium-sized snake lizards are found in a wide variety of habitats throughout Australia. They feed on insects and other arthropods. It is possible that at least two species from this genus mimic venomous snakes which occur within their range (see page 70).

The genus *Aprasia* consists of nine species of very small snake lizards. None of them grows to more than about 20 cm (8 in) in total length and most are restricted to dry sandy soils, although they may also be found beneath stones. Several species are known only from a handful of specimens, possibly because they are easily overlooked due to their small size. The least known of all snake lizards, however, is *Ophidiocephalus taeniatus*. Until recently, only a single specimen of this lizard had been found, and it is the only member of its genus.

The genus *Lialis* consists of two large snake lizards, one from Australia and New Guinea, the other endemic to New Guinea. The Australian species, Burton's small lizard, *L. burtoni*, grows to 60 cm (2 ft) or more and occurs in a variety of colour forms, ranging from plain cream or pale yellow to dark brown, with or without a pattern of stripes or spots. A cream or white line commonly runs from the tip of the
to the eye and

Plate 69. A large species of snake lizard, *Pygopus lepidopodus.*

greatly elongated snout, which is wedge shaped and tapers to a sharp point. The eye is large and the species is not inclined to burrow, but hunts terrestrial lizards, especially skinks, but also geckos. Its pointed snout is thought to be an adaptation to the swallowing of proportionately large prey because, like snakes, these species are obliged to swallow their food whole. The species from New Guinea, *L. jicari,* is similar in appearance and habits.

The genus which gives its name to the family, *Pygopus,* consists of only two species, although these have a collective range which covers the whole of Australia. *P. nigriceps* is found in the north and centre of the country and is mainly nocturnal, whereas *P. lepidopodus* (Plate 69) is found in the south and south-east and is diurnal. Both these species are quite large, growing to a snout–vent length of 18 cm (7 in) and 23 cm (9 in) respectively, and they are primarily insectivorous. *P. nigriceps* may also be a snake-mimic.

Plate 70. *Anolis carolinensis* is native to North America, but has been replaced in several localities by introduced species. ▶

IGUANIDAE – Iguanas

NUMBER OF SPECIES: Approximately 650

DISTRIBUTION
North and South America including the West Indies and Galapagos Islands, Madagascar, Fiji and Tonga.

Many iguanids are large, brightly coloured and adorned with crests, dewlaps and other ornamentation, but others are small, brown and

rather plain in appearance. Throughout their large range they occupy a wide range of habitats, from deserts to rain forests, mountains to the coast, and one species is the closest any lizard comes to being truly marine.

Their distribution is interesting because their presence in Madagascar, Fiji and Tonga illustrates a number of principles of animal dispersal and speciation (see Chapter 7).

The largest genus by far is *Anolis*; more than 110 species occur on the West Indian islands alone, and there are another 40 or so species in Mexico. Many more are found in other parts of Central and South America, while one species is native to North America. Anoles are quite easy to distinguish from other lizards. They are streamlined, with long tails, long legs and digits and a narrow head. In males (and females of some species) there is an erectable throat fan, which varies in colour from species to species but is invariably brightly coloured. This is lowered during encounters with other lizards and forms an important aspect of their display repertoire. Anoles are usually brown or green in

Plate 71. The Cuban anole, *Anolis sagrei*, one of several West Indian lizard species which have been introduced to Florida, where they quickly establish themselves in urban environments, living on the walls of houses, in ornamental shrubs and patio plants, as shown here.

colour, and many species are able to change their colour rapidly, an ability which has led to the (misleading) local name of 'chameleon' for some species. Most are about 20 cm (8 in) in total length, although a few species, notably *A. equestris* from Cuba and *A. richardi* from Tobago, grow to about twice this length. They occupy a number of ecological niches from the ground to the tree-tops, and the way in which species 'share' a habitat by varying their niches has provided important evidence in the science of community ecology. Briefly, where more than one species occur together in an area, each will tend to use a different part of that habitat, so avoiding undue competition for resources. For instance, one species may live on the ground, another on tree-trunks and a third in the canopy. There may also be differences is size and prey type. Even within species, males and females often differ in size and/or micro-habitat and so avoid intra-specific competition.

There can be no doubt that anoles are among the most successful of all lizards; population densities of up to 20,000 per hectare have been estimated for certain islands, the highest densities so far recorded for any species (see Chapter 7). Even in places where several other lizards live, anoles are usually the most conspicuous species, and are frequently seen around houses and other buildings. Unfortunately, some species are so successful that they have a habit of displacing native species if they are accidentally or deliberately introduced. For instance, the Cuban species *Anolis sagrei* has established itself in at least two parts of Florida and occurs in unbelievable numbers in surburban habitats (Plates 47 and 71) – the native *Anolis carolinensis*, which used to be common in these areas, can now no longer be found and, more worrying, the Cuban species is beginning to spread out into some of the more natural habitats. In addition to this species, Florida natives have to contend with three more 'illegal immigrants': *A. equestris*, the knight anole, which is a large species, also from Cuba; *A. cybotes*, the large-headed anole; and *A. distichus*, the bark anole, both from Hispaniola.

The biology of *Anolis* species has probably been studied in greater detail than any other group of lizards. One of the more interesting findings is that most, perhaps all, species do not actively thermo-regulate, but allow their body temperatures to rise or fall according to the ambient temperature. This is to be expected in the case of forest species because they do not have opportunities to bask, but many anoles live in open habitats and yet still make no attempt to maintain a stable body temperature. Their reproduction is also interesting. Nearly all species lay a single egg at a time (a few of the large ones may lay up to three), but lay at regular intervals during the breeding season, which may extend throughout the year in favourable environments. This strategy of laying many small clutches is also found among the geckos, but is not typical of any other iguanids, as far as is known.

In North and Central America, the genus *Sceloporus* contains a variety of lizards known collectively as swifts or spiny lizards. Many of these are associated with the drier regions of the American south-west, but other species range down into the more humid regions of southern Mexico

and Guatemala. As their common name suggests, the spiny lizards have pointed scales which give them a spiky appearance. Some species, such as the crevice spiny lizard, *S. poinsetti*, use their spiny tails to protect them when they retreat into cracks, and several others, such as Yarrow's spiny lizard, *S. jarrovii* (Plate 72) are also associated with rocky habitats. The latter species is live-bearing, a characteristic shared by other montane species, e.g. *S. malachitus* from Central America. Most of the lowland species lay eggs. Male spiny lizards are often brightly coloured during the breeding season, but females are drab brown or grey. *Uta stansburiana*, the side-blotched lizard, and *Urosaurus* species, the tree lizards and brush lizards, are similar in form to *Sceloporus* but do not have the long spiny scales. These small lizards can be very numerous in certain habitats. The reproductive habits of the side-blotched lizard have been extensively studied and some populations are thought to be virtually annuals, the adults breeding throughout the summer and dying before the next breeding season, when a new generation takes over. Each female may lay up to seven clutches per year, and the average clutch size varies according to the rainfall, which, in turn, controls the food supply.

Other North American iguanids are desert adapted. The most extreme examples of these are the horned lizards, *Phrynosoma* spp., all 14 of which are found in the drier regions of the United States and Mexico.

Plate 73. *Urosaurus microscutatus*, a small iguanid, in a typical basking posture on the trunk of a cardon cactus in Mexico.

127

Horned lizards are sometimes called horned 'toads' due to their toad-like shape (the Latin name *Phrynosoma* means 'toad-bodied'). They vary slightly in size but, typically, grow to about 15 cm (6 in) in total length. A rim of backward-pointing spines projects from the back of their head and most species have a row of spines around the flanks. Their coloration is a beautiful example of camouflage, consisting of disruptive markings on a background which matches the substrate on which they live (Plates 2 and 35). Several species also have a pale vertebral stripe which further breaks up their body outline. Among their unique features, several of which have been mentioned elsewhere, are their extremely rounded shape, their diet of ants and the ability of some species to squirt blood from their eye-sockets. Horned lizards regulate their body temperature by shuffling into the sand or soil in order to avoid extremes of temperature. Their first activity in the morning is to force their head above the surface. By exposing their head to the sun they warm their brain, and also transfer heat to other parts of the body via the blood circulation, in readiness for complete emergence. Early morning basking often involves flattening the body and tilting it towards the east in order to maximise the effects of the rising sun. Most lay eggs, which can number up to 45 per clutch in the Texas horned lizard, *P. cornutum*, but one species, the short-horned lizard, *P. douglassi*, which lives in cooler regions than the others, gives birth to about 20 living young.

Other species of iguanids found in the North American deserts include *Uma notata*, a pale-coloured lizard which lives among sand dunes. Its toes are fringed with modified scales, which help it to run across the loose surface at incredible speeds, and its snout is wedge-shaped, enabling it to dive into the sand, competely burying itself once it has out-paced its pursuers. Two other species of *Uma* occur in the American south-west, one of which, the Coachella Valley fringe-toed lizard, *U. inornata*, is endangered due to the loss of much of its habitat.

The lesser and greater earless lizards, *Holbrookia maculata* and *Cophosaurus texanus*, are similar in general body form. A population of *Holbrookia* which lives among the dunes of White Sands in New Mexico consists of pale, almost white, individuals (Plate 37). *Cophosaurus* raises its tail if it is approached, exposing a series of black and white bands, before it runs away. A similar strategy is employed by the zebra-tailed lizard, *Callisaurus draconoides*, which occurs further west.

Also found in this region is the desert iguana, *Dipsosaurus dorsalis*, a species which grows to about 30 cm (12 in) and is unusual among North American iguanids in eating vegetation, especially the leaves and stems of the creosote bush. The chuckwallas, *Sauromalus*, are also large herbivorous species, but they are restricted to rock outcrops and rocky mountainsides. One species, *S. obesus*, occurs in the United States and others are found in Mexico. These lizards retreat into rock crevices if they are threatened and then, by inflating their bodies with air, resist all attempts to dislodge them.

Moving further south, a number of large iguanids begin to appear. These include the spiny-tailed iguanas, *Ctenosaura*, of which several species are found in Mexico and Central America. They are large ground-dwelling species which occupy a range of habitats from semi-arid scrub to forests, and are often found in the vicinity of villages and settlements. They are replaced in the West Indies by the rhinoceros iguanas, *Cyclura*. Altogether, eight distinct species are recognised, several of which are further subdivided into sub-species. These huge, gnarled lizards live among rocks and scrub, where they feed mainly on vegetation. They are dull in colour, usually brown, and their head is ornamented with small horns and dewlaps. They are all restricted in their ranges which include, collectively, Cuba, Hispaniola, Jamaica, the Cayman Islands and the Bahamas. Due to habitat destruction, especially by feral goats, and to predation by introduced cats, dogs and rats, all species and sub-species of *Cyclura* are endangered and most, if not all, will become extinct in their natural habitat by the turn of the century. A few species are bred regularly in captivity, although numbers are so small that the danger of inbreeding could be a potential problem.

On the Galapagos Islands there is a number of small iguanids, but these are completely overshadowed by three large species. Two of these, *Conolophus subcristatus* and *C. pallidus*, are terrestrial. They are found on separate islands (*C. pallidus* is found on Barrington, the other species is more widely distributed throughout the islands), and almost certainly evolved, not too long ago, from the same ancestors. These species are large, heavy-bodied animals which feed mainly on the fruits and leaves of prickly pear cacti (*Opuntia*).

The marine iguana, *Amblyrhynchus cristatus*, is one of the most interesting of all lizards. This species feeds only on marine algae (seaweed) which grow in the shallow seas around the islands. In order to graze successfully, it must expose its body to the low temperatures of the water for extended periods of time and this is achieved by a physiological 'trick' explained in Chapter 3. In addition, they have nasal glands in their nostrils, which concentrate saltwater and then expel it in a shower by snorting. Adaptations for swimming are the partially webbed feet and a tail which is flattened from side to side. When they are not feeding, the iguanas congregate on the rocks and cliffs along the shore, where the females and juveniles often lounge about on top of one another, forming large heaps, and the males space themselves out and maintain small basking territories. Their skin is often invaded by ticks, which are sometimes removed by crabs.

The well-known common, or green, iguana, *Iguana iguana*, is found on the mainland of South and Central America and on Trinidad and Tobago as well as several of the smaller West Indian islands. A closely related species, *I. delicatissima*, is also found on several of the Lesser Antilles. The green iguana is large, up to 2 m (6.5 ft) including the tail, and impressive, with a single row of enlarged tooth-like scales forming a dorsal crest, and a heavily folded dewlap. Coloration varies between individuals, and may be grass green or blue-green, sometimes suffused with orange-brown. Males establish large territories and warn off intruders by raising their body and nodding their head vigorously.

Plate 74. A common iguana at home in an Ecuadorian forest. It can be seen in the centre of the picture, and is displaying to a neighbouring male.

The animal illustrated in Plate 74 habitually surveyed his territory from the top of a tree, as shown, and frequently displayed to a neighbouring male who was established in another tree-top about 100 m (109 yd) away. Occasionally he would descend from his tree to feed among the surrounding vegetation. Female iguanas lay large clutches of eggs, which they bury in sandy soil. The young measure about 20 cm (8 in) on hatching, and some reports suggest that they eat the faeces of adult iguanas; it has been suggested that this innoculates their gut with the bacteria necessary to help them digest the cellulose in their diet. Young iguanas probably eat a certain amount of insect food, but as they grow they become almost exclusively herbivorous.

From the same part of the world come the basilisks, *Basiliscus* spp., and these, like the green iguana, inhabit the banks and margins of streams and lakes. Several species are recognised, of which the plumed basilisk, *B. plumifrons*, is one of the more spectacular. Basilisks rarely reach 1 m (3 ft) in total length and have long hind legs and a long tail, two characteristics which combine to enable them to run rapidly on their hind legs if necessary, sometimes skimming across the surface of water in order to escape from predators.

Polychrus is a genus of slow-moving arboreal iguanids which are active mainly at night. They are frequently found in shrubs and bushes, relying on their excellent camouflage, rather than speed, to escape notice, and can be thought of as New World counterparts to the chameleons (although they are not so elaborately adapted as those lizards).

Uracentron flaviceps is another arboreal iguanid from South America, although its appearance is not in keeping with other arboreal species. It is a heavy-bodied lizard, growing to about 20 cm (8 in) with a short, spiky tail. Its coloration is spectacular; the tail and body are black, the head is pale orange with black flecks and there is a pale pink collar. Few of these lizards have been found, since they live only in tall trees in the rain forest, and little is known of their natural history except that they are probably insectivorous.

The genera *Plica* and *Enyalioides* are also rain forest species, and are slender lizards with long tapering tails and long digits. *Plica plica*, which has no common name, habitually rests on vertical surfaces with its head pointing downwards, and even sleeps in this position.

Several genera of small to medium-sized iguanids inhabit Central and South America, including 'general-purpose' lizards such as the curly-tails, *Leiocephalus*, which are rather similar in their appearance and life-style to the *Sceloporus* species found further north. However, the Andes Mountains are the home of a number of species which are adapted to withstand extremes of temperature and long dry periods. The small *Tropidurus* species are found throughout the range and are typically ground and rock-dwelling, and are sometimes known as lava lizards. Other, more specialised, lizards belong to the genera *Vilcunia, Liolaemus, Diplolaemus* and *Centrura*. These are typically heavy-bodied lizards, often with spiny tails. Species from very high altitudes are often very dark in colour, to enable them to absorb solar radiation efficiently. Others, such as *Centrura patagonica*, are obese-looking species which store fat beneath their skins in readiness for droughts. Many of these species are live-bearing, again an adaptation to life in a cold climate, but egg-layers are also represented. Many of the species are variable in colouring, depending on the geology of the region they inhabit. As far as is known, all are insectivorous in diet.

One of the peculiarities about iguanid distribution is their presence on Madagascar in the Indian Ocean. This fact provides good evidence for the continental drift theory, and also indicates that iguanids were formerly more widespread than they are today. Seven species occur on the island, one in the genus *Chalarodon* and six in *Oplurus*. *C. madagascariensis* is a sand-dwelling species; the *Oplurus* species are arboreal (two species) or rock-dwelling (four species). Three of these four have flattened heads, as seen in other rock-crevice-living lizards, but the fourth, *O. quadrimaculatus*, is more generalised. A sub-species of *O. cuvieri* also occurs on the offshore island of Great Comoro. Other than this, the natural history of these lizards is not well known.

The iguanas of Fiji and Tonga, however, are better documented. They probably arrived on the islands by rafting, and are clearly related to the Galapagos iguanas, the Galapagos archipelago being situated in the same ocean current as the Fiji/Tonga group. *Brachylophus fasciatus* was described as long ago as 1800 (as *Iguana fasciata*). It is found on several widely separated islands of the Fiji group, and grows to about 75 cm (2.5ft) in total length. It is bright green with broad pale blue bars and has a dorsal crest consisting of a row of conical scales (Plate 31). *B. vitiensis*, by contrast, was not discovered until 1981, mainly because it has a much more limited distribution (the small island of Yaduataba, part of the Fiji group). It is somewhat similar to *B. fasciatus* in appearance but is slightly larger and its bars are white with black borders. Both species are arboreal and herbivorous, and both lay small clutches of eggs in holes which the female excavates. These eggs have an abnormally long incubation period (about eight months in *B. vitiensis*), and the hatchlings are about 25 cm (10 in) in length. On the nearby island of Tonga, a similar species, *B. brevicephalus*, is found.

Plate 75. *Agama atricollis*, an arboreal agamid from Africa.

SUMMARY

In summarising this large and important family of lizards, the most striking characteristics are their diversity, both in size and shape, and in life-style. Included among them are species which have adapted to extremes of climate and habitat, from the deserts of south-western North America to the rain forest of Central and South America and the semi-marine environment along the coasts of the Galapagos archipelago. As will be seen in the next section, the radiation of the iguanids in the New World has been closely paralleled by the agamids in the Old World, to the extent that several pairs of species are almost indistinguishable without close scrutiny. In addition to their past evolution, it seems that some groups of species, notably the anoles, are still in a state of evolutionary flux, with species expanding and contracting their ranges constantly, and recently established populations, for instance on islands, rapidly becoming different from their parent stock. At the other extreme, unfortunately, are the groups of species, such as the rhinoceros iguanas, which are experiencing a rapid and precipitous decline – these are obviously the losers in an evolutionary sense, although their fate has undoubtedly been accelerated by human impact on their tiny refuges.

AGAMIDAE – Agamids

NUMBER OF SPECIES: Approximately 300

DISTRIBUTION
Africa (except Madagascar), Central, South and South-East Asia, Australia, one species in Europe.

The agamids are the Old World counterparts of the iguanids. They parallel them in many aspects of their biology and general appearance, but are distinguished from them by a different arrangement of the teeth. Although the agamids had a wider distribution in the past, there is no part of the world today where both families co-exist.

In common with the iguanids, they are well endowed with crests, frills and flaps, and males of many species are brilliantly coloured. Some species, such as *Physignathus*, the water dragons, and *Chlamydosaurus kingii*, the frilled lizard, are capable of bipedal locomotion. The larger species, like *Hydrosaurus*, the sail-finned lizards, may reach almost 1 m (3 ft) in length, but most agamids are medium sized, typically about 30 cm (12 in). The great majority are insectivorous, but the mastigures, *Uromastyx* spp., from North Africa and the Middle East, are entirely herbivorous. A few other species, such as the larger species of bearded dragons, *Pogona* (formerly known as *Amphibolurus*), also eat some vegetable material.

All species are oviparous, with the exception of those belonging to the genus *Phrynocephalus*, the toad-headed lizards, and *Cophotis ceylanica*, the prehensile-tailed lizard from Sri Lanka. *Liolepis belliana*, an Asian species, may be parthenogenic.

In Africa, the most conspicuous species are those belonging to the type genus *Agama*. *Agama agama* is often known as the rainbow lizard, but males of all species are brightly coloured and have the ability to intensify their colour and markings during territorial or courtship displays. A characteristic shared by a number of species is a bright electric-blue head, which gives an unmistakable signal when it is bobbed rapidly during these displays. The females and juveniles, however, are cryptically coloured, usually in shades of brown or grey, and often with a paler vertebral stripe which helps to break up the visual outline of the lizard. These lizards frequently live above ground level, and the various species favour vantage points such as tree-trunks or rocks, although they may forage on the ground for their food. Other species are almost entirely terrestrial, and some, such as *A. etoshae*, a southern African desert species, retreat into burrows to avoid unsuitable temperatures or predators.

A single species of *Agama* is the family's sole representative in Europe. *A. stellio* (Plate 27) is found on several Greek islands as well as in parts of South-West Asia and North Africa. It lives in localised colonies and often perches on the tops of dry stone walls, rapidly retreating into crevices if approached.

The genus extends well into Asia, and a number of species are found in the Indian region. A range of habitats is utilised by the various species and some are found at very high altitudes, e.g. up to 3,300 m (11,000 ft) in the case of *A. himalayana*. In addition to these lizards, Asia is the home of an assortment of agamids of every shape, size and colour. Most numerous are the *Calotes* species, sometimes known as garden lizards. These are arboreal lizards with laterally compressed bodies, long slender tails and, in the case of males, a distinct dorsal crest consisting of enlarged tooth-like scales. *C. versicolor* is probably the most familiar species, from India and Indo-China north into Afghanistan and China. It is predominantly brown in colour, although a red area around the head and throat of breeding males has earned it the name of 'bloodsucker'. This and some other species of *Calotes* are also known locally as 'chameleons' due to their ability to change colour rapidly, although their repertoire is rather limited compared with that of their namesakes. Other species, such as *C. cristatellus*, from the Malayan peninsula and Indonesian islands, are permanently bright emerald green in colour, often with white undersides, and are among the most elegant of lizards.

South-East Asia is also the home of the celebrated flying lizards, *Draco*, of which about 40 species are recognised. These agamids are remarkable for the wing-like structures which are formed from a membrane of skin stretched over the ribs, six or seven of which are hugely elongated. When at rest, the lizard folds these back along its flanks, but in 'flight' they are extended at right angles to the body, forming a pair of gliding wings (Fig. 5). Overshadowed by the wings, but no less remarkable, is the possession of large pendulous wattles and

the exception of *Physignathus leseurii*, which has close relatives in South-East Asia. This is a large water dragon which is usually found in trees along water courses or on the coast. It grows to around 70 cm (28 in) total length and is greyish with a series of dark and light bars along its back and flanks (Plate 78). *Caimanops amphiboluroides* is a small terrestrial species from Western Australia and *Chelosania brunnea* is a medium-sized species which is notable for its chameleon-like habits; it is an arboreal lizard which moves slowly and relies heavily on camouflage. *Moloch horridus*, the thorny devil, has already been dealt with at some length in connection with its diet, its adaptation to a desert environment and its convergent evolution with the North American *Phrynosoma* species (page 93). It is largely confined to the arid regions of the interior of the continent.

The frilled lizard, *Chlamydosaurus kingii* (Plate 40), is one of Australia's most celebrated species. It occurs in the northern part of the continent (and in southern New Guinea) and lives in woodlands and scrub. It is mainly arboreal in habit but descends to the ground to feed and, if approached at this time, goes through its repertoire of intimidation by erecting the large ruff around its neck, standing on its back legs and making off bipedally.

SUMMARY

To summarise this family of lizards, it becomes obvious that there are close parallels between it and the iguanids. These two families are assumed to have come from a common ancestor and become split up through the activities of continental drift. Radiation into different environments has occurred in both groups of lizards, leading to many remarkable examples of convergence of forms and habits.

CHAMAELEONIDAE – Chameleons

NUMBER OF SPECIES: Approximately 85

DISTRIBUTION
Africa, Madagascar, South Asia, southern Europe.

If there is one group of lizards which can be identified by anyone, it is the chameleons. They are unlike any other reptiles and, like the camel, appear to have been designed by a committee. In fact, chameleons as a group are probably the most perfectly adapted lizards ever to have evolved – their form and life-style are uncompromisingly committed to an arboreal existence and to this end there is hardly a single part of the body which is not radically modified.

Their trunk is excessively flattened from side to side, a shape which helps them to absorb radiation during the early and late portions of the day, but avoid it during the hottest times. It also enhances their

Plate 79. *Chamaeleo oustaleti*, from Madagascar, is probably the largest species in the family.

camouflage, and is ergonomically suited to climbing along thin branches. Their tail is prehensile, and when not in use is usually coiled like a clock spring, and their feet consist of two opposed sets of fused digits for gripping with. The head is large and often domed, or casqued, and may carry ornamentation in the case of males, consisting of crests and/or horns which are sometimes used in combat. The eyes are large, but almost entirely covered with skin, leaving only a small central aperture for viewing. The eyes can be moved, gun-turret-like, independently of each other so that the lizard can look in two directions at the same time. Finally, the tongue can be extended to a length equal to the chameleon's body and terminates in a muscular and sticky tip with which insects and other prey are captured.

The quality for which the chameleon is most famous, having been mentioned as long ago as the third century BC by Aristotle, is its ability to change colour. As it happens, this talent is probably its least understood and most exaggerated quality! Although it is true that they have a good repertoire of colours and patterns, these are more associated with light intensity and sexual and territorial display than with camouflage and, in any case, they are by no means the only lizards which are able to alter their colour. Changes in markings are brought about by altering the distribution of pigment granules in specialised colour-giving cells, the chromatophores, in the skin. This is not done instantaneously but may take several minutes, since it is achieved by the release of hormones into the blood circulation. The number of colour schemes open to an individual chameleon is limited by the presence or absence of various pigments, but usually includes several shades of green and brown. A few species, notably the dwarf chameleons, *Bradypodion*, have streaks and flecks of pink and purple along their flanks, especially during the breeding season.

All chameleons are extremely non-social. Although they tend to be found in discrete colonies, males and females space themselves out by displaying aggressively to other individuals, opening their mouths wide, inflating their bodies and hissing. Males may interlock their horns and attempt to dislodge their opponent, and may eventually resort to biting.

There are 25 species of chameleon living in Madagascar, but they have been little studied here. These include some of the largest, such as Parson's chameleon, *Chamaeleo parsoni* (Plate 24), which grows to well over 40 cm (16 in) total length and eats small vertebrates as well as insects; the largest of all chameleons, *C. ousteleti* (Plate 79), a predominantly brown species which has been reported up to 63 cm (25 in) in length, and another large species, *C. pardalis*. On the other hand, some Madagascan chameleons, such as *C. nasutus*, are so small that they are preyed upon by orb-weaving spiders and praying mantids.

A number of more familiar species is found on the African continent. These include Jackson's chameleon, *Chamaeleo jacksoni*, a spectacular species in which the males have three ridged horns (Plate 20). This species is found from lowland forests to quite high elevations on the flanks of Mount Kenya, where individuals are significantly bigger and more brightly coloured. In southern Africa the flap-necked chameleon, *C. dilepis*, is the most ubiquitous species. Whereas Jackson's chameleon gives birth to living young, this species lays up to 50 eggs, the female descending from the branches to dig a tunnel in which to deposit them.

The Namaqua chameleon, *C. namaquensis*, another egg-laying species, is unusual among chameleons in spending much of its time on the ground. As a result, its tail is not as prehensile as that of other chameleons, although it is still used when climbing. This chameleon lives in the arid south-western region of Africa where the only vegetation is in the form of scrub, and it hunts for beetles, rodents and

Plate 80. The sail-finned chameleon, *Chamaeleo montium*, from West Africa, is a medium-sized species in which the males have two horns on their snouts.

other lizards. Although it bears no horns, it is a distinctive species due to the row of knobs which form a crest along the ridge of its back.

Chamaeleo montium, from West Africa (Plate 80), is sometimes known as the sail-fin chameleon because of its raised dorsal crest. This is a more moderately sized species which has two horns and a wide selection of colours and patterns.

The single species of chameleon from India and Sri Lanka is *C. zeylanicus*. This is a green species without horns, which grows to about 20 cm (8 in). The females lay about 30 eggs. Two other species live in Asia but are restricted to the Arabian peninsula, and a single species reaches southern Europe. This is *C. chamaeleon*, the 'common' chameleon. Its hold in Europe is somewhat tenuous since it is found in only a few localities in extreme southern Spain and on the island of Crete. It also occurs in North Africa, from whence it undoubtedly spread across the Straits of Gibraltar, and in the Canary Islands.

The so-called 'dwarf' chameleons, formerly included in the genus *Chamaeleo*, are now regarded as a separate genus, *Bradypodion*. They are nearly all restricted to southern Africa where a large number of different species or races are found, most of them occurring only in a small area. Differences between them are slight and of interest only to a taxonomist. The dwarf chameleons all lack horns or crests, although they have high casques covering their necks. All species are live-bearing and may give birth to several broods thoughout a single season. The babies are extremely tiny, but grow rapidly and can be sexually mature within a year. Male dwarf chameleons are especially colourful and display spectacularly to females and to rival males.

The leaf chameleons comprise two genera: *Brookesia* from Madagascar and *Rhampholeon* from East and southern Africa. These are diminutive chameleons which live in montane rain forests. They are not nearly as colourful as the larger species already dealt with, usually being some shade of brown, and the males lack horns or crests, although the snouts of some species are angular. They are characterised by short tails, and their common name comes from their resemblance to a dead leaf with a short stalk.

LACERTIDAE – Wall Lizards and related species

NUMBER OF SPECIES: Approximately 200

DISTRIBUTION
Most of Europe, Asia and Africa (excluding Madagascar).

The lacertids form a fairly well-defined group of species which may be thought of as 'typical' lizards: they have cylindrical bodies, long tails and powerful legs, the hind pair of which are longer than the front pair. The dorsal scales are small and granular, whereas those on the underside are rectangular and plate-like. There is frequently sexual dimorphism, the males of many species being brightly coloured, especially during the breeding season when they become highly territorial and aggressive towards one another. The tail is easily discarded, and may be brightly coloured in some species. All lacertids lay eggs, with the exception of the European common lizard, *Lacerta vivipara*, which is the most northerly occurring species, extending up into the Arctic Circle.

The most ubiquitous European genus is *Podarcis*, the members of which are usually referred to as wall lizards. About 15 species are found on the continent, with several others just outside the area. Of these, many are divided into a multitude of sub-species, some of which should be regarded as dubious, but there is no doubt that those species which occur on small islands, for instance in the Mediterranean, demonstrate island sub-speciation to a high degree (see Chapter 7). The best-known species is *P. muralis*, the archetypal 'wall' lizard, found in a variety of forms throughout much of central and south-eastern Europe. This species and *P. sicula*, the ruin lizard, often occur in huge numbers on old stone walls, buildings and along roadsides, where they are conspicuous by virtue of their bright colours and basking activities. In other parts of Europe they are replaced by equally common, but more restricted species, such as *P. hispanica* in Spain and *P. erhardii* and others on the Balkan peninsula. On the islands of the Mediterranean are found a number of interesting species, many of which are colourful. The Balearics, Sardinia and Corsica, the Adriatic Islands and the Aegean Islands all have endemic species, some of which are illustrated in Plates 54, 55 and 82. All of these species lay small clutches of eggs, usually three to six, and many of them, especially those from southern Europe, lay several clutches throughout the year. The young are drab-coloured,

Plate 81. A European wall lizard, *Podarcis muralis*, from Italy.

like the females, and the male coloration is not attained until they are sexually mature. Green is the most common colour among the members of this genus, although some species and sub-species are blue (Plate 56). Among island forms there is a tendency towards melanism.

The closely related genus *Lacerta* has a similar range and its members are similar in appearance. A few, however, grow to a larger size than any of the *Podarcis* species. These include *Lacerta lepida*, the eyed lizard or jewelled lizard of south-western Europe and North Africa, which grows to a potential 80 cm (31 in) in total length and feeds largely on vertebrates, including smaller species of lacertids, and the green lizards, *L. viridis* and *L. trilineata*, which are slightly smaller.

Of the smaller species, the common, or viviparous lizard, *L. vivipara*, is the best known since it has a huge range over most of central and northern Europe, as well as extending far into Central Asia. These small brown lizards are found in a range of habitats including meadows, heaths and moors and in many places they are the only reptiles present. They give birth to small dark-coloured young at the end of the summer, and hibernate for up to six months during the colder parts of the year.

The sand lizard, *L. agilis*, also has an extensive range throughout Europe and Asia, but is limited in the north by its egg-laying reproductive mode. This species has a variety of colour forms. Throughout most of its range it is beige with a broken black band down the centre of the back, the males developing brilliant green flanks during the breeding season, but in parts of the range a proportion of the population has a solid reddish-brown back. The remaining members of the genus have fairly restricted ranges, often in upland or montane situations, where they replace the more warmth-loving *Podarcis* species.

The other European lacertids are placed in smaller genera such as *Algyroides*, *Psammodromus* and *Acanthodactylus*. All of these, however, show the usual lacertid conformation, although they may have minor adaptations such as the heavily keeled scales of *Psammodromus* or the fringed toes of *Acanthodactylus*.

Lacertids are comparatively rare in Asia, but are, once again, rather similar in appearance to the species already described. The genus *Ophisops*, which just ranges into Europe, is here represented by four or five species, which are notable for their fused eyelids; the lower one covers the eye permanently and the lizard sees through a transparent area forming a window. For this reason they are known as snake-eyed lizards. Other common genera are *Takydromus*, of which one species, *T. sexlineatus*, has a huge range throughout much of the continent, and *Eremias*, of which about 45 species and numerous sub-species are known. The members of both these genera prefer open habitats such as grassland, steppe and semi-desert, although some are found in mountain foothills.

The African genera of lacertids include some more specialised kinds, including desert-adapted and arboreal species. They are present in fair numbers in the north of the continent, mainly species belonging to genera which are also present in Europe such as *Acanthodactylus* and *Lacerta*. (It seems likely that the family evolved in Africa and spread north across the Straits of Gibraltar and round the eastern shore of the Mediterranean.) Several species live around the fringes of the Sahara Desert, once again demonstrating their preference for open habitats.

A number of genera are present in southern Africa, including several with a single species. These include the specialised desert form, *Aporosaura anchietae*, from the Namib Desert, which lives among sand dunes, eating insects and wind-blown seeds, and retreating beneath the surface to escape from intense heat during the middle of the day. Another highly adapted species is *Holapsis guentheri*, an arboreal species with a bright blue tail. This lizard is reported to leap from tree to tree, using its broad tail to stabilise it in flight, and this ability is probably enhanced by a frill of large scales around the margin of the tail.

Plate 82. Milos wall lizard, *Podarcis milensis*, one of dozens of small lacertids found throughout southern Europe and the Mediterranean islands.

provides shelter and hiding places, and where they find an abundance of food in the form of spiders, beetles, caterpillars and cockroaches. Leaves and fruit make up a small proportion of their food. Jungle runners are normally brown in colour, although males may develop bright green flanks, especially during the breeding season. Females lay clutches of two to six eggs which are buried in sand or loose soil. Lizards of the genera *Kentropyx* and *Teius* are rather similar in size and appearance, although they are often more brightly coloured; *K. pelviceps*, for instance, has a wide bright green stripe from its snout to the base of its tail.

A small number of teiids are much larger, approaching the size of the Old World monitor lizards. For example, the tegu, *Tupinambis teguixin*, grows to almost 1 m (3 ft) in length. This South American lizard is an active predator and scavenger which lives in or around forest clearings, but is also occasionally seen around houses and villages. Its diet also includes some plant material. It has small shiny scales and is brown or black in colour with ragged crossbars of white, cream or yellow. *T. rufescens* is slightly larger, although it has a more restricted range, being confined to the Chaco region of northern Argentina and adjacent countries. Its habits are otherwise similar to

Plate 84. The six-lined racerunner, *Cnemidophorus sexlineatus*, a typical small teiid from North America.

those of *T. teguixin*, and these two species are the only members of the genus now that *T. nigropunctatus* is thought to be merely a local form of *T. teguixin*.

The caiman lizards, *Dracaena guianensis* and *D. paraguayensis*, are semi-aquatic teiids growing to 90 cm (35 in). Their common name is derived from the large knobbly scales which cover the back, resembling those of crocodiles and alligators. Their colour is dull brown or olive, with faint paler mottling on the flanks. Males develop an orange and black throat. They live in the vicinity of rivers and streams and feed almost exclusively on marsh snails of the genus *Ampullaria*, crushing the shells with their powerful jaws and specially flattened teeth. *Crocodilurus* is another macroteiid with a preference for aquatic or semi-aquatic habitats.

Several other less conspicuous genera of teiids are found in South America and the West Indies – these are classified as microteiids – and although they often have Old World counterparts, they do not parallel any one family in particular. *Bachia* species are unusual in having their limbs reduced almost to nothing (there is no lacertid counterpart to this form) and the scales arranged in regular bands running around the body. They are very small burrowing species which are occasionally found beneath rotting logs, etc., and which feed mainly on soft-bodied invertebrates such as worms and insect larvae. *Ptychoglossus* is also elongated, with small limbs, but the degree of reduction is not so great. The genus *Arthrosaura* shares the annular arrangement of scale rows with both of these genera, but its limbs are of more normal proportions. *A. kockii* has unusual markings; its body is brown except for a wide orange dorsal stripe which gradually widens on the lower part of the body and extends onto the tail which is completely orange.

Members of the genera *Alopoglossus* and *Leposoma* are small species which have heavily keeled scales on their backs and flanks. They all forage through leaf-litter, feeding on a wide variety of small insects, including ants and crickets, and spiders. There appears to be a constant clutch size of two eggs in these species. *Neusticurus* is similar in size, but raised scales form four ridges down the back, giving it a superficial resemblance to the much larger caiman lizard, and this species also appears to be restricted to waterside habitats. However, its food, consisting of insects and other small lizards, is terrestrial.

Three genera of South American microteiids are very skink-like in appearance, having large glossy scales and a cylindrical body. These are *Iphisa*, *Tretioscincus* and *Gymnophthalmus*. *Iphisa elegans* has an unusual arrangement of two longitudinal rows of very large overlapping scales down its back. *Gymnophthalmus* species have a collective range from Trinidad and Venezuela in the north down to Argentina. This genus, along with one other, *Pantodactylus*, is sometimes placed in a separate family, the Gymnophthalmidae. Although there are several other small genera of teiids in South and Central America, their biology is not well known.

Plate 86. *Tiliqua gigas*, one of the large skinks known as 'blue-tongues'. This species is from New Guinea, whereas the others are Australian.

With the exception of a single species, *T. gigas*, which is found only in New Guinea and Indonesia, all ten species are Australian. Four of these are commonly known as blue-tongued skinks: *T. multifasciata*, the central blue-tongue, *T. nigrolutea*, the blotched blue-tongue, *T. occipitalis*, the western blue-tongue and *T. scincoides*, the eastern blue-tongue. All are large (to about 50 cm/20 in total length), heavy-bodied skinks, with a massive head and a short tail. As their common name suggests, they are distinguished by a bright blue tongue, which is rolled forward in their open mouth if they are threatened by a potential predator or if the males encounter rivals. They give birth to litters of ten to 25 relatively large young once each year. Blue-tongued skinks are diurnal, and omnivorous in their feeding habits, eating a wide range of insects, snails, carrion, fruit and leaves. The pink-tongued skink, *T. gerrardii*, is similar but much more slender. This species is partially arboreal and is unusual in feeding almost exclusively on land molluscs. It, too, gives birth to live young, but has larger litters (and smaller young) on average than the other species. All of these species are boldly marked with crossbands or blotches. The remaining *Tiliqua* species are smaller and more elongated.

Plate 87. A typical skink, of the genus *Mabuya*, from west Malaysia. The numerous Asian species in this genus are not easily told apart in the field.

Closely related to *Tiliqua*, and sometimes included in that genus, is the stump-tailed skink, *Trachydosaurus rugosus*. This species grows to about 30 cm (12 in) in total length, and is heavily built with a broad head and short, flattened tail. Its most characteristic feature is the covering of huge rough scales, frequently likened to those of a fir-cone, and reflected in its alternative name of shingle-back. Several races are known and these vary in colour from jet black all over to dull brown with scattered white, yellow or orange spots, especially on the flanks. Its activity pattern and feeding habits are like those of the blue-tongues, but it differs in its breeding habits, giving birth to one, two or three very large young.

Egernia is a large genus with over 20 species in Australia and one in New Guinea. Its members can be divided roughly into two groups: rough-scaled species which live among rocks, and smooth-scaled species which are found in forests, grassland and deserts. Of the former group, *E. cunninghami* is one of the most familiar. It is highly variable in colour and may be plain brown or grey, or it may have a pattern of paler markings arranged into indistinct cross-bands. This rock-crevice lizard has sharply pointed, keeled scales, and is therefore spiky in appearance. It is omnivorous and gives birth to about five live young. *E. hosmeri* is a similar species, but rather more heavily built. *E. depressa* and *E. stokesii* are than most and grows to about 25 cm (10 in) total length. It is completely black and has a large range, taking in most of the Pacific island groups, from the Solomons to Fiji, Tonga and Samoa. Whereas most of the species in this genus have a constant clutch size of two eggs, *E. nigra* lays up to four.

Among the more unusual skinks from this region are those of the genus *Tribolonotus*, the members of which have heavily keeled, spiny scales, giving them a most un-skinklike general appearance. These are associated with damp habitats in rain forests, often living alongside streams. Most lay clutches of a single egg, but *T. schmidti* from Guadalcanal gives birth to one living youngster. Very similar, both in habits and appearance, are the skinks belonging to the genus *Tropidophorus*, one species of which is found in tropical regions of Australia, the remainder being scattered throughout the Philippines, the Indonesian archipelago and southern China.

Yet another bizarre skink from the same region is *Fojia bumui*, the only member of its genus, which comes from New Guinea. It has a strange arrangement of scales, which are large and plate-like down the centre of its back, but granular on its flanks. Although few specimens have been studied, it is apparently restricted to stream-side habitats, where it clings to vertical rock faces waiting for food to swim, crawl or fly past. At night it climbs into low bushes and sleeps on a leaf.

Skinks of the genus *Prasinohaema* are unique among reptiles in having a green blood pigment. This makes their tongues and the inside of their mouths green also, and their eggs, of which two are laid, are also green. There is no known explanation for this odd arrangement. All five species, which are found in New Guinea and the Solomon Islands, are highly arboreal, bright green in colour and have adhesive toe-pads, just like those of some geckos, enabling them to climb smooth surfaces.

The Solomon Islands are also the home of what is probably the largest of all skinks, *Corucia zebrata*, a highly arboreal species with several unique characteristics. It grows to a total length of about 70 cm (28 in) and is unusually heavily built for an arboreal lizard (Plate 33). It is slow-moving and largely nocturnal in habits, and feeds exclusively on vegetation. It has a thick muscular tail which it uses when climbing (the only skink to do so), and only rarely descends to the ground. It gives birth to a single, very large, living youngster. It is the only member of its genus, and its relationships with other skinks are not clear.

In South-East Asia and the Indian region the skink fauna is equally rich, but very many of them are insufficiently studied and much work remains to be done before they can be accurately accounted for. Wide-ranging genera such as *Tropidophorus* are still present, whereas others are either restricted to the region or extend eastwards into Africa and Europe. *Mabuya* is an important genus, of which about 85 species are known, 20 of them in India and Indo-China, and the rest scattered throughout the Pacific region, on islands in the Indian Ocean and in Africa and South America, making it the most cosmopolitan of all skink genera. These species are fairly typical, being moderate in size with well-developed legs (Plate 87). Most are brown, although a number of species have brightly coloured tails. The two species living on the Seychelles Islands, *M. sechellensis* and *M. wrightii*, have already been referred to at length in connection with their unusual feeding ecology (page 56). In southern Africa, skinks of this genus are conspicuous diurnal insectivores. A number have brightly coloured tails, e.g. *M. quinquetaeniata*, the African five-lined skink. *Mabuya* contains both egg-laying and live-bearing species as well as some species which can do both – two common southern African forms, *M. varia* and *M. capensis*, lay eggs in part of their range but give birth to live young elsewhere. This intra-specific variation epitomises the versatility of the skink family.

Other major genera from this part of the world include *Riopa* from India, the Middle East and North Africa. These are mostly small species with reduced legs. They live in sand, soil or leaf-litter and their glossy scales make them difficult to catch or hold. Most are brown in colour but a few have brilliant red flanks and these are sometimes known as fire skinks. *Lygosoma* is a closely related genus of 30 to 40 species, including some which were formerly placed in the previous genus. They are also slender, cylindrical species with slightly reduced legs. Most are brown or yellowish-brown to match the soil on which they live and in which they burrow, but some, e.g. *L. simonettai* from Somalia, are quite colourful.

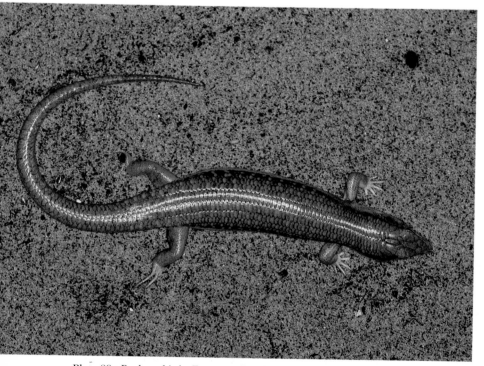

Plate 89. Berber skink, *Eumeces schneideri*, from North Africa. This attractive species is the largest in the genus. It lives in burrows on the fringes of deserts.

Plate 90. A North American skink, *Eumeces laticeps*. Only males have the bright orange heads, the colour being intensified during the breeding season by increased levels of the male hormone, testosterone, in the blood.

As far as is known, all are insectivorous, and both egg-laying and live-bearing species are known.

In North Africa and the Middle East a number of skinks are known as sandfish. These are species with reduced or absent legs, which specialise in living in loose wind-blown sand dunes, hunting their prey, in the form of insect larvae, etc., under the surface. All have smooth shiny scales and a pointed or wedge-shaped snout and are pale brown to yellow in colour (Plate 5). These belong to a range of genera such as *Ophioscincus*, *Scincus*, *Sepsoides* and *Sphenops*, and represent a case of convergent evolution among themselves as well as with members of other families such as the two *Anniella* species from similar habitats in North America. The species with small legs may use these occasionally when progressing slowly above the surface, but when moving quickly or tunnelling the limbs are laid along the body, where they fit into recesses, and the lizard moves by wriggling rapidly from side to side, hence the name sand 'fish'.

Southern Africa constitutes the entire range of a highly distinctive group of skinks comprising the sub-family Acontiinae. The 17 species have lost all trace of limbs and they have short blunt tails. All are burrowing lizards which spend the larger proportion of their lives below the ground, feeding on worms and other soft-bodied invertebrates. Life-history details are unknown for many of them, but, as far as is known, all give birth to living young. Seven species belong to the genus *Acontias*, including the largest species in the family, *A. plumbeus*, which grows to 55 cm (22 in) in total length. This species occasionally takes small vertebrates in addition to worms, etc., and gives birth to a dozen or more live young. It is uniformly black or dark grey in colour, but several other species are attractively striped in dark brown on a yellowish background, or have their scales edged in black to give a tessellated pattern. The woodbush legless skink, *Acontophiops lineatus*, is the only member of its genus and differs from the *Acontias* species in having fixed eyelids with transparent windows.

The remaining species of this sub-family, included in the genus *Typhlosaurus*, have scales covering their eyes and it is doubtful whether they can see at all. They are known, therefore, as blind legless skinks. The nine species are found in desert or semi-desert habitats where they hunt insect larvae and termites beneath the surface. They are typically yellow or pale brown in colour, with several longitudinal stripes. Some are known only from a few specimens, but some species, at least, give birth to one or two relatively large young.

Other legless skinks in southern Africa belong to the more widespread sub-family Scincinae, and include several species in the genus *Scelotes*, known as the burrowing skinks. This genus also contains a number of species with reduced, but functional, legs and so, once again, it is possible to demonstrate progressive leg loss within a closely related group of animals.

Exactly the same progression can be seen in the genus *Chalcides*, which is widely distributed throughout North Africa, southern Europe and the Middle East. The most extreme form is *C. guentheri*, which has tiny vestigial limbs with no digits, but other species, such as *C. bedriagai* from Spain and Portugal and *C. ocellatus* from south-eastern Europe, North Africa and parts of western Asia, have well-developed limbs with five digits all round. The longest species, *C. chalcides*, from southern Europe and North Africa, can grow to 40 cm (16 in), of which the tail makes up about half. This is an intermediate form, in which the limbs are short but end in three digits. It is not a burrowing species but lives in dense vegetation, especially meadow-grass. (As a matter of interest, this species was the 'original' skink described by Linnaeus, and named from the Greek word *kalcides* which referred to a bronze-coloured snake.) Although several of the *Chalcides* species are common and familiar lizards in the regions where they occur, three are enigmatic, only single specimens of each having been collected. Two other genera occur in Europe, both represented by a single species. *Ophiomorus punctatissimus* is the Greek legless skink, growing to about 20 cm (8 in), and *Ablepharus kitaibelii* is the snake-eyed skink, so called because its eyelids are fused, the lower one having a transparent window in it. Both are secretive species which spend much of their time beneath stones or logs, or buried in leaf-litter. Both genera are also represented in western Asia by small numbers of additional species.

The genus *Eumeces* has a large range spanning the Atlantic Ocean. Six or more species are found in Asia, the Middle East and North Africa, the most impressive being the Berber skink, *E. schneideri*, from desert fringes of North Africa (Plate 89). These large and attractive skinks grow to 30 cm (12 in), live in burrows and apparently eat carrion as well as insects and small vertebrates. The main contingent of the family, however, is found in North America, where 12 species are found in the United States and several more range down into Central America. A characteristic of many of the American species is the bright blue or red tail, which is most prominent in young animals but may also be present in adults of certain species (Plate 41). In other respects, the *Eumeces* skinks are typical in appearance, with well-developed legs, shiny scales and a pattern which consists largely of longitudinal cream stripes on a dark brown background. The largest species is *E. laticeps* (Plate 90), which is sometimes known locally as the 'scorpion', as are several species in Mexico and Central America, where they are widely believed to be poisonous. This group of skinks is of interest because females of some species brood their eggs; small clutches of about three to seven eggs are laid beneath a log or stone and the female curls around them during the incubation. There is some evidence that she may move them if the conditions in the nest become unfavourable. Other species do not show this type of parental care, and these lay rather larger clutches on average, while one species, *E. callicephalus*, gives birth to living young in the montane parts of its range and lays eggs near the coast. Similarly, three montane species of *Eumeces* from Mexico all give birth to living young.

Two other genera of skinks are found in North America, both containing a single species. These are *Scincella lateralis*, the ground skink, a small species growing to about 10 cm (4 in) which is found throughout most of eastern North America, and *Neoseps reynoldsi*, the sand skink, reaching aproximately the same size but differing in having very reduced legs. This species is restricted to areas of loose sand and is a 'sand-swimmer'. Due to its specialised habits and habitat, it has a far more restricted range than *Scincella* and is found only in two small areas of Florida. Both these species are insectivorous and lay eggs.

The skinks are poorly represented in South America, where only eight species, belonging to the genus *Mabuya*, are found in the whole region, including the West Indies. These all have the appearance typical of the genus, and are mostly brown or bronze in colour, with cream stripes. The most widespread species, *M. mabouya*, is found in forest clearings and gives birth to four to six live young.

CORDYLIDAE – Girdle-tailed Lizards, Plated Lizards and related species

NUMBER OF SPECIES: Approximately 70

DISTRIBUTION
Endemic to Africa and Madagascar.

The cordylids include the 70 or so species which go under the common names of girdle-tailed lizards, zonures, plated lizards and rock lizards. The family is restricted to Africa and Madagascar, and its members are especially numerous in southern Africa. Although they are typically insectivorous, several of the large species also eat some vegetable material, including fallen fruits and berries and lichen. They inhabit rocky terrain or open grassland – none appears to be arboreal. The tails of most species are fragile, although the girdle-tailed lizards use theirs as defensive weapons and are less prone to part with them than some of the other species. Both live-bearing and egg-laying species are found in this family.

Members of the type genus, *Cordylus*, are the girdle-tailed lizards or zonures. All species have sharply pointed scales around the rear of the head and on the tail. These latter scales are arranged in regular rings or 'girdles' which give the lizards one of their common names. Along the back the scales are rectangular in shape and arranged like roof tiles to give a good degree of protection. Most girdle-tailed lizards are rock-dwellers which, typically, live among the granite outcrops, or 'kopjes' of southern Africa. The largest species, however, *Cordylus giganteus* (Plate 91), prefers more open situations and is found in grassland, where each individual digs a long burrow which forms the centre of its home range and its night-time retreat. This species can grow to 30 cm (12 in) or more and uses its heavily armoured tail as a weapon as well as to plug the entrance to its burrow. It frequently basks on a prominent hummock such as a termite mound, and its posture has led to the local name of 'sungazer'. *Cordylus cataphractus*, the armadillo lizard, is a

Plate 92. A large plated lizard, *Gerrhosaurus major.*

according to its locality; the sub-species *T. a. africanus* has tiny front and hind limbs, whereas *T. a. fitzsimonsi* has no front limbs at all.

The two remaining mainland genera have only one species each. *Cordylosaurus subtessellatus* is a small brightly coloured rock lizard from south-western Africa. Its body is marked with broad cream and chocolate-brown stripes, while the tail is brilliant blue – a colour scheme which recurs often throughout the lizard kingdom. *Angolosaurus stoogi* is a highly specialised 'sand-swimmer' which lives in and on the sand dunes of the Namib Desert. It has a short tail, a wedge-shaped snout and a powerful body, all of which help to push it rapidly through the sand. The back is pale in colour, nearly white, with many small pinkish-red spots. The chin and throat are deep glossy black. Because of its almost sterile habitat, this species is catholic in its diet, eating insects, vegetation and even windblown seeds.

The genera *Tracheloptychus* and *Zonosaurus* occur on Madagascar. The latter is rather like a medium-sized plated lizard, but more colourful, with two black-edged buff stripes running along the body

Plate 93. The undersides of male *Platysaurus* lizards are brilliantly marked, but are visible only when the lizard displays.

from the snout. Little is known about the natural history of any of these lizards.

DIBAMIDAE – Blind Lizards

NUMBER OF SPECIES: 10

DISTRIBUTION
One species, *Anelytropsis papillosus*, lives in north-eastern Mexico, the other nine (genus *Dibamus*) are found in South-East Asia, from Indo-China and the Malayan peninsula, Indonesia and the Philippines to New Guinea.

The blind lizards are strange burrowing animals which are not at all well known. Various experts have suggested that they are most closely related to the geckos or the skinks. Others think that they are closer to the amphisbaenians or even the snakes. Apart from the widely separated ranges of the two genera, they suffer from extreme rarity – most species are known from less than 20 specimens.

They are small, being less than 20 cm (8 in) in total length, and cylindrical in shape. Being totally adapted to an underground existence, their eyes are completely covered with scales and all species have lost their front limbs; rudimentary hind limbs, consisting of a flipper-like stump, are present only in the males. Most of the specimens which have been found have been discovered by lifting rotting logs, etc., although the Mexican species is apparently more tolerant of dry conditions.

Their breeding biology is virtually unknown, except that there is an old record of an egg containing a fully developed embryo of *Dibamus alfredi*, which was found in Thailand. The egg was unusual in that its shell was brittle and calcareous, like those of geckos. Several preserved specimens of *D. novaeguineae* also contains a single egg in their oviduct, as does a female *Anelytropsis*.

ANGUIDAE – Glass Lizards, Alligator Lizards and related species

NUMBER OF SPECIES: Approximately 75

DISTRIBUTION
North and South America and the West Indies. Europe, including Britain, Middle East, South and South-East Asia.

This is a varied family with a number of distinct groupings. Most anguids are heavily scaled, almost armour-plated, and many have a pleat or fold along each flank which allows for distention of their otherwise inflexible skin when they are carrying eggs or have eaten a large meal. The family includes both egg-laying and live-bearing forms, sometimes in the same genus (e.g. *Elgaria*). One genus, *Ophisaurus*, is found in both the New and Old Worlds.

There is a strong tendency within this family for limb reduction or loss. The alligator lizards are fairly conservative in this respect, but the West Indian genus *Diploglossus* contains species which seem to be in the process of losing their limbs, while the slow-worm, *Anguis fragilis*, and the glass lizards, *Ophisaurus* spp., have no limbs at all. Most species are terrestrial, but again there is great variation. Some, such as the slow-worm, are semi-burrowing, while others, such as the Central American *Abronia* species, are arboreal. The European glass lizard, *Ophisaurus apodus*, is probably unique among lizards in being the only legless species to climb, although it must be said that it restricts its arboreal tendencies to basking in low shrubs, from which it can quickly descend if disturbed. All species are carnivorous, their exact diets often depending on their size. Animals eaten include insects, small mammals, other lizards and land molluscs.

167

Plate 94. The Texas alligator lizard, *Gerrhonotus liocephalus*, an anguid with fairly well-developed legs.

Those North American species with legs are known as alligator lizards; until recently, they were all placed in the genus *Gerrhonotus*. Most have now been removed to *Elgaria*, leaving only the Texas species, *G. liocephalus*, where it was. Superficially, the alligator lizards are similar. They grow to about 30 cm (12 in), sometimes slightly more, and are slender lizards with long tails. The scales are large and squarish in shape, giving them their common name, and they are brown or grey in colour, often with indistinct cross-bars of black and white. Four of the five species lay eggs, numbering up to 20 per clutch, but the most northerly occurring species, *E. coeruleus*, gives birth to live young. Alligator lizards are typically slow-moving and, although found in some of the most arid regions of North America, they tend to inhabit wooded valleys and other humid microhabitats.

The 18 species of *Diploglossus* are known as galliwasps, and several of them grow quite large; *G. warreni*, which comes from Haiti, grows to 45 cm (18 in) and eats nestling rodents and birds as well as insects. They live in a variety of terrestrial habitats, including rock outcrops, and show a gradation in limb reduction. Most are found on the islands of Hispaniola and Jamaica, with one species on each of Cuba, Puerto Rico and Montserrat. The tree-dwelling *Abronia* of Central America are often found in epiphytic bromeliad plants in the upper layers of the rain forest, and have long prehensile tails (a trait which seems to be present to some degree in some *Elgaria* species).

Ophisaurus is represented by three species in North America, one which ranges from south-eastern Europe into western Asia and two in southern Asia. All are legless and are commonly known as glass lizards or glass 'snakes' due to the readiness with which they part with their tails. All species lay eggs and feed on insects and soft-bodied invertebrates, including slugs and snails. The North American species are rather similar in appearance, being brown with darker longitudinal stripes (Plate 4), these stripes being more prominent in juveniles. The eastern glass lizard and the slender glass lizard, *O. ventralis* and *O. attenuatus*, grow to around 100 cm (39 in), but the island glass lizard, *O. compressus*, only reaches about half of this size. They are secretive lizards, most often found beneath logs, boards and other items

Plate 95. The European slow-worm, *Anguis fragilis*. The male is uniformly coloured, whereas the female has a thin vertebral line. Both of these specimens have damaged tails, that of the male most recently.

of junk which humans thoughtfully leave lying around for the use of reptiles. The European species is rather larger, growing to 120 cm (47 in), but is similar in colour and markings, except for juveniles, which are pale grey with dark brown crossbars. Compared to the North American glass lizards, the European species is less retiring and frequently basks in the open or among the branches of low bushes. (In the Balkan region of Europe, glass lizards are so common and conspicuous in the grazed roadside meadows that it is often possible to spot them from a moving car.) The two Asian species of *Ophisaurus* are not well known, but are thought to be similar to *O. apodus* in habits and appearance.

The other completely legless genus is *Anguis*, which has only one member, the slow-worm, *A. fragilis*. This species is found throughout most of Europe, western Asia and a small portion of North Africa. The slow-worm is much smaller than the glass lizards, averaging about 25–30 cm (10-12 in) in total length, but is similarly coloured in various shades of brown. It is usually found beneath objects, often in moist situations, although it occasionally emerges to bask during the day. Although it is popularly thought to favour slugs, its diet includes many invertebrates and also small vertebrates such as other species of lizards, if it gets the chance. Unlike the *Ophisaurus* species, the slow-worm gives birth to live young, litters numbering from six to twelve or more.

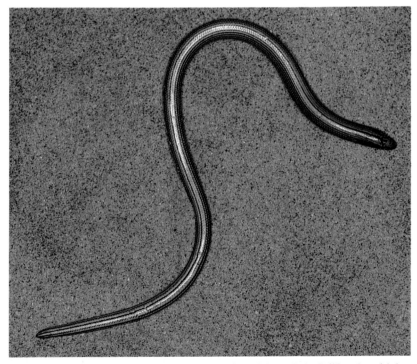

Plate 96. *Anniella geronomensis*, a tiny legless lizard from Baja California, which swims through sand.

ANNIELLIDAE – Legless Lizards
(Note: the members of this species are sometimes included in the Anguidae.)

NUMBER OF SPECIES: 2

DISTRIBUTION
California and Baja California, Mexico. Both species are confined to narrow strips of land adjacent to the Pacific coast.

Both of these legless lizards are small shiny snake-like animals, but with movable eyelids. They are secretive lizards, living in sand, soil or leaf-litter, and are rarely seen. They are able to move rapidly through the loose substrate, and appear to spend most of their time around the root systems of the sparse plants which share their specialised habitat (Plate 97). They emerge onto the surface at night, and feed on small invertebrates, presumably above and below ground. Both species give birth to a small number of living young (one or two in *Anniella geronomensis* and one to four in *A. pulchra*).

Plate 97. The coastal dune habitat of *Anniella*, near San Quintin, Mexico. The lizards only venture onto the surface at night and are otherwise found only in the sand, especially around the roots of the equally specialised plants which share their habitat.

XENOSAURIDAE – Xenosaurs

NUMBER OF SPECIES: 4

DISTRIBUTION
Mexico, China.

The family Xenosauridae consists of just four species living in widely separated parts of the world. All four species are viviparous, producing four to seven live young, but otherwise almost nothing is known of their natural history. The Chinese crocodile lizard, *Shinisaurus crocodilurus* (Plate 98), is a semi-aquatic lizard with a double crest of enlarged scales running down its back. Apparently, it lives in cool forest areas and spends much of its time in shallow water or in overhanging branches and vegetation. Its diet includes fish and tadpoles.

The genus *Xenosaurus*, with three species, is confined to eastern Mexico. Its members live in mountainous regions, both in dry scrub and in rain forest. It appears to be mainly insectivorous in diet, and is nocturnal.

Plate 98. Chinese crocodile lizard, *Shinisaurus crocodilurus*, the only Asian member of its family, the other three being found in eastern Mexico.

VARANIDAE – Monitors

NUMBER OF SPECIES: Approximately 30

DISTRIBUTION
Australasia, South East-Asia and Africa.

The monitors (commonly known as leguaans in Africa and goannas in Australia) belong to a family which has a single genus, *Varanus*. Included in it are a number of large and spectacular lizards, including the largest in the world, *Varanus komodoensis*, the Komodo dragon. The greatest amount of radiation has taken place in Australia, where there are also more species than in the rest of the range combined. Two species are restricted to Africa and the remainder are found throughout South-East Asia and the Pacific region. Characteristics of the family are their well-developed limbs and deeply forked tongues which are continually flicked out like the tongue of a snake when the lizard is active. All species are carnivorous and are active foragers, their prey depending very much on their size, and ranging from termites and other insects to moderately large mammals. Carrion is also taken, at least by the larger species. They tend to swallow their prey whole, but large carcasses are sometimes ripped apart, often by several lizards feeding at the same time. In parts of their range, monitor lizards fill the ecological niche which is more commonly thought of as belonging to predatory and scavenging mammals – this may account for their success in Australia and on some of the Pacific islands, where mammals of this type are absent. All monitors lay eggs, sometimes using termite mounds as incubation chambers.

At least 20 species occur in Australia of which 17 are endemic. The others are also found across the Torres Strait in New Guinea and neighbouring islands. An additional species, *Varanus salvator*, is widespread throughout South-East Asia and the Indo-Pacific region, and may just reach the northernmost tip of Australia.

The largest Australian species is the perentie, *Varanus giganteus*, which may grow to 2.5 m (8 ft), although on average it is smaller than this. This huge lizard lives around desert fringes, expecially where there are rocky outcrops in which to hide. *V. varius*, the lace monitor, grows almost as long as the perentie, but is rather less heavily built. This is in keeping with its arboreal habits, for the lace monitor specialises in robbing birds' nests, patrolling a large territory and systematically examining hollow trees and stumps for occupants. Like other large monitors, however, it also takes reptiles, small mammals and carrion. Gould's monitor, *V. gouldii*, is the third Australian 'giant' monitor, and occurs in a range of habitats over almost the whole continent. This species is remarkable for the way in which it uses its tail as a third leg when it raises itself up to survey its surroundings. A recently described species, *V. panoptes*, is similar to Gould's monitor and grows to 1.2 m (4 ft).

Several of the Australian monitors reach a size of around 1 m (3 ft),

173

including a number of interesting species. *V. spenceri* lives in open grassland and hides in burrows – it is a generalist and feeds on a variety of small animals – while *V. glebopalma* is a secretive species which lives among rocks and hunts mainly during the evening. Other Australian monitors reaching 1 m (3 ft) include two aquatic species, *V. mertensi*, which is endemic, and *V. indicus*, which is also found throughout much of New Guinea and the Indonesian archipelago. These species include animals such as fish and frogs in their diet, in addition to insects, nestling birds and small mammals. They have flattened tails which improve their ability to swim, but they also climb into waterside plants and trees, especially mangroves. Two slightly smaller, but equally aquatic, species are *V. semiremex* and *V. mitchelli*, both endemic to Australia and having a maximum size of around 60 cm (2 ft).

In the same size range are two highly arboreal species, *V. prasinus* and *V. timorensis*. Both have the largest parts of their ranges outside Australia and are found mainly in New Guinea and neighbouring islands – *timorensis* is obviously found on the island of Timor also. *V. prasinus* is an attractive species which occurs in two colour phases: normal specimens are bright green in colour with a series of indistinct darker crossbars, but a totally black (melanistic) form is also found. This species is remarkable for its extreme slenderness and its long narrow head and neck. It is found in a variety of tropical habitats, including rain forests and mangrove swamps. Both these species are essentially tropical in their distribution, but a third arboreal species, *V. tristris*, is found thoughout Australia, except in the most southern parts. This is a variable species, but often has a totally black head and neck. In addition to trees, it may also climb among rocks in the more arid parts of its range.

The remaining species are all under 1 m (3 ft) in total length, and it is only in Australia that small species of monitors such as these are found. This is probably due to the lack of several lizard families which are found elsewhere, enabling these smaller monitors to take the place of species such as the collared lizard in North America and the eyed lizard in Europe, for instance. *V. acanthurus* grows to 60 cm (2 ft) and is restricted to desert environments, where it lives among rock outcrops and feeds mainly on smaller lizards and insects. The remaining species may be loosely called 'pygmy monitors' since none of them are over 50 cm (20 in) in total length. *V. brevicauda* is the short-tailed monitor. It grows to only 20 cm (8 in) and is a desert species, feeding largely on small lizards. *V. eremias* is slightly larger, growing to 40 cm (16 in), but shares the same range and habitat as the previous species, whereas two other pygmy monitors, *V. gilleni* and *V. caudolineatus*, are semi-arboreal. The remaining Australian species are small rock-dwelling species which have restricted ranges in the north of the country. These are *V. glauerti*, *V. kingorum*, *V. pilbarensis*, *V. primordius* and *V. storri*. All are rare and live in an inaccessible region, and their natural history is not well known. They range in size from 25 to 40 cm (10–16 in) and are primarily lizard and insect eaters.

Over two-thirds of the world's monitors, then, have been recorded in Australia, and they fill a wide variety of ecological niches left open to them by the absence of several families of lizards, predatory and scavenging mammals and, to some extent, predatory birds. In other parts of the family's range, monitors are less diverse and tend to be the largest lizards present. In Asia the most widespread species is the water monitor, *V. salvator*, which has a huge range taking in the whole of the Indonesian archipelago, the Malayan peninsula, Indo-China, Sri Lanka and the Bay of Bengal region. It is usually associated with water, although it is by no means strictly aquatic in habit and may be seen crossing roads and scavenging around villages and plantations over much of its range. It also occurs along the shore-lines of coasts and estuaries and has been seen swimming far out to sea. It grows to a maximum of 2 m (6.5 ft), although it is more typically about half this size, and it is drab grey or olive in colour with indistinct yellow mottling. The markings of the young are much more striking since they are darker in overall colour with spots of yellow arranged into transverse stripes. This species is hunted in various parts of its range, both as food and for its skin.

Varanus komodoensis, the Komodo dragon, is easily the best-publicised monitor lizard. It has been the subject of an extensive scientific study as well as a television series and accompanying book (see bibliography). Apart from the small island of Komodo, it also lives on two even smaller islands in the Indonesian chain, Padar and Rinca, and on part of neighbouring Flores. Komodo itself is a national park, the only case of an area set aside specifically to protect a lizard. Young Komodo dragons feed on the usual insect and small mammal fare, but adults are capable of bringing down and dismembering deer and pigs, which form their main prey. In addition, large specimens are known to prey on young of their own species. Human visitors to the islands have been known to fall prey to the lizards on several, well-documented occasions, and it seems likely that local villagers have also been taken from time to time over the years. The situation is made worse at present due to the type of protection which the lizards are given – tourists are encouraged to bring an animal carcass to a feeding station in order to attract them and this has gradually led to the absence of the normal fear that lizards have for humans. Nobody would deny that such an interesting and spectacular animal should enjoy strict protection, but its use as a means of parting tourists from their money not only degrades the animals but may be seriously interfering with their long-term prospects.

Varanus salvadorii, Salvador's monitor, is found in New Guinea. It may grow as long as the Komodo dragon but is less bulky. Very little appears to be known of the natural history of this species.

Moving on to the less celebrated species of Asian monitors, *V. bengalensis* (Plate 99) occurs throughout India, Sri Lanka and Burma and is known as the Bengal monitor. It grows to about 1.5 m (5 ft) in length and is grey or olive with darker blotches. These prefer drier habitats than *V. salvator*, and are found in forests as well as around

175

Plate 99. Bengal monitor, *Varanus bengalensis.* (Photograph courtesy of Stephen Peltz.)

villages. *V. nebulosus*, the clouded monitor, is found in the Malayan peninsula, Thailand and Burma and grows to slightly more than 1 m (3 ft) in length. Its habits are similar to the preceding species, which replaces it further north, although it is not as common. *V. dumerili* is a fairly rare species which lives mainly in coastal mangrove forests on the Malayan peninsula and Indo-China, especially on small islands. *V. flavescens* is found in northern India and neighbouring countries, where it is restricted to dry, semi-desert habitats. It grows to slightly less than 1 m (3 ft), but is uncommon and little is known about its natural history.

One monitor, *V. griseus*, links the Asian species with the African ones. This species is known as the desert monitor, and is found in suitable habitats from northern India west through the Caspian region and into North Africa. This is a large species, growing to well over 1 m (3 ft), which prefers open country with little or no vegetation. It retreats into burrows and feeds on other desert animals – rodents, snakes, lizards and insects. It is pale grey, brown or yellowish-brown in colour and has dark crossbars along the back and tail. As usual, juveniles are more strikingly marked than adults. Apparently, 15 to 20 eggs are produced, buried in the sand or laid at the end of the burrow.

Two monitors are found south of the Sahara in Africa. The most common is the Nile monitor, *V. niloticus*, which is found from Egypt down the Nile valley and into eastern, central and southern Africa. It is a large species, growing to 2 m (6.5 ft) and is quite colourful for a monitor, being grey or olive in colour with numerous white or yellowish ocelli, and darker blotches on the back and limbs. Old individuals may

chew on the victim, are potentially fatal to humans, although reports of fatalities are rare. Fortunately, the beaded lizards are secretive and retiring animals which rarely interact with people in the normal course of their lives. The Gila monster is legally protected throughout that portion of its range which lies within the United States.

The most famous (or infamous) species, *Heloderma suspectum*, is found in the Sonoran, Mojave and Great Basin Deserts of north-western Mexico and Arizona, spilling over into small parts of New Mexico, Nevada, Utah and California. Although not a rare species, it is secretive, spending the greater part of its life below the ground in a burrow, and is therefore often overlooked, even in areas where it is common. This is all the more surprising when its coloration, consisting of bright salmon pink bands or reticulations on a jet black background, is considered. It grows to 50 cm (20 in) in total length, making it the largest lizard in the United States as well as the only venomous one.

Gila monsters have a well-defined seasonal activity pattern. They emerge from hiberation in January or February and spend the first few weeks near their hibernation chamber or den. Courtship and mating take place from late April until early June and the three to eight eggs are laid about two months later. These eggs overwinter beneath the ground and hatch the following spring, the incubation period being around ten months. The hatchlings are about 16 cm (6 in) in length, and are well equipped with venom (and quite prepared to bite) as soon as they emerge. Their markings are often brighter than those of the parents, and the pink areas take the form of solid wide bands around the body and tail. As they grow, these markings are broken up by the incursion of black, resulting in a more or less reticulated adult pattern, depending on sub-species (the form known as *H. s. cinctum* has a tendency to retain the basic juvenile pattern of bands).

After egg-laying, the adults spend gradually less time on the surface in order to avoid the hottest part of the summer, although they are sometimes active during the evening. By November they will have returned to their regular hibernation site.

Because the rather restricted diet consisting of nestling animals, ground nesting birds and birds' eggs. They are opportunistic feeders which probably manage on very few meals each year, but when a food source is found it is fully exploited. Adults can consume up to 35 per cent of their body weight in one sitting; juveniles slightly more. Prey is found mainly by scent, their olfactory sense being highly developed. Once prey is located, the Gila monster uses its powerful legs and long claws, if necessary, to dig down until it is reached.

The Mexican beaded lizard, *Heloderma horridum*, is a much larger animal, reaching a maximum length of 90 cm (35 in). Its range covers much of the western coastal region of Mexico, south to Guatemala. It is darker in colour than the Gila monster, and its few markings are white, cream or pale yellow. Juveniles are more boldly marked, with yellow spots, blotches and bars and five or six light bars around the tail. A sub-species from the region of Chiapas in Mexico and northern Guatemala,

H. h. alvarezi, is totally black in colour when adult, although the juveniles are similar to those of the nominate sub-species. Although the Mexican beaded lizard lives in a hot region, it is not confined to deserts as is the Gila monster, and is more often found in dry scrub and light woodland. The range of *H. h. alvarezi*, in particular, coincides with an area of fairly high humidity.

This species has a similar diet to that of the Gila monster, although birds' eggs and fledglings may be proportionately more important. Feeding takes place mainly in the rainy season and the lizards are inactive during the hottest and driest months of the year (which may vary from one part of their range to another). This species lay more eggs, on average, than the Gila monster, probably due to the larger size of the females. Clutches of 15 have been recorded, although ten is probably more normal. *H. h. alvarezi* is smaller in size and lays fewer eggs, usually four or five. The eggs are commonly laid over a period of several days, and the embryos may be partially developed at the time of laying.

LANTHONOTIDAE - The Bornean Earless Monitor

NUMBER OF SPECIES: 1

DISTRIBUTION
Borneo

The Bornean earless monitor, *Lanthonotus borneensis*, is not a true monitor, but is placed in a separate family, the Lanthonotidae. It is intermediate between the beaded lizards and the true monitors in appearance and undoubtedly comes from the same line of descent as those two families.

It differs from its close relatives in not possessing ear openings or venom glands, and by having its nostrils situated on top of its snout rather than at each side. Its eyes are small, but it has sensory pits, the precise function of which are unknown, in some of its larger scales. *Lanthonotus* must rate as one of the most enigmatic of all lizards. Despite its importance in understanding the evolution and relationships of the varanoid lizards, so few specimens have been found that almost nothing is known about its habits or natural history. It appears to be adapted for swimming and for burrowing, and may live in murky ditches and swamps. Its movements on land are clumsy, and it appears to be unable to use its legs to any great effect, progressing by wriggling its body from side to side, snake-like. It seems to eat a range of animal material, including fish and egg-yolk, and uses its long tongue to examine food and its surroundings. Apparently it lays eggs, but other details of its reproduction are not yet known.

Chapter 10

The Amphisbaenians

NUMBER OF SPECIES: 130 in four families

DISTRIBUTION
North and South America, Africa, western Asia and the Middle East, extreme southern Europe.

The amphisbaenians form a separate sub-order, Amphisbaenia, within the order Squamata. They are therefore not lizards, nor are they snakes, although they are assumed to have arisen from a common ancestral line. They are included here because they are a fairly small collection of species which would otherwise be overlooked. They are sometimes known as 'worm-lizards', a misleading term which is probably best avoided, although it is difficult to think of an appropriate alternative, except the rather clumsy term amphisbaenian (pronounced 'am-fis-bay-nee-an').

Four families are recognised, but they are not easily distinguished on superficial characteristics, excepting for one of them (Bipedidae), which is described below. All amphisbaenians are characterised by the annular arrangement of their skin and scales, and their tiny eyes, which are covered with scales and are therefore inconspicuous. This gives them the appearance, at first glance, of an earthworm. The similarity is not coincidental, either, because these reptiles are unique in being exclusively burrowing in their habits, and spend almost their entire lives beneath the ground. They live in burrow systems which they construct themselves, using their specialised heads to drive a tunnel through the soil, which may be quite hard in some instances. The soil is then compacted by movements of the skull; these movements can be up and down or from side to side, according to the species. The animal moves along its tunnel by sliding its rings of skin forward, over the body itself, bracing them against the walls of the tunnel and then pulling the body forward by means of muscles connecting the body wall to the inside surface of the skin.

Although digging can be a slow and laborious process, once a tunnel system is constructed, the amphisbaenian can move through it rapidly, and may locate itself within the system according to the temperature of various sections, i.e. if they are in the sun or in the shade, or how close to the surface they are. At night they may emerge onto the surface in order to feed, although they are normally only seen if heavy rains have flooded their burrows and forced them out. Food is probably obtained in at least three ways: invertebrates such as earthworms and insect larvae may enter a section of tunnel by accident; the tunnel system may extend into an area of sand or soil which includes a nest of insects such as termites or ants; or the amphisbaenian may move to the surface, or to a part of the burrow just beneath the surface, in order to ambush invertebrates and small vertebrates which pass by – they appear to be highly sensitive to the slightest movement overhead, and react rapidly by breaking through the surface, when necessary, in order to grasp their prey.

They also have enemies, and these consist largely of snakes which track them along their tunnels. In South and Central America, a number of the venomous coral snakes, *Micrurus*, appear to specialise in this method of hunting, and may constitute the main predator in some places. In Africa, quill-snouted, purple-glossed and wolf snakes probably fill the same niche in places where amphisbaenians are common. Some amphisbaenians are capable of discarding the end section of their short blunt tail, like some lizards, although they are unable to grow a replacement and so the strategy can be used only once.

Some amphisbaenians lay eggs, others produce living young. Eggs are sometimes laid in ant or termite nests, where temperature and humidity are kept fairly stable by the insects, and the proximity of a ready supply of food for the newly hatched reptile may also be a consideration, but very little is known about what goes on under the ground.

AMPHISBAENIDAE

The largest family is the Amphisbaenidae, found in South America, Africa and southern Europe. The ability to autotomise varies throughout this family; there is a tendency for the smaller species to be able to discard their tails, whereas larger ones do not.

The largest species are those belonging to the genus *Amphisbaena*, such as *A. alba*, a stocky, plain white animal growing to about 75 cm (30 in). It is found throughout northern South America, including the island of Trinidad, in suitable habitats. It lives in tropical rain forests and is frequently found inside the huge nests of leaf-cutter ants, possibly using these nests for egg-laying. It has powerful jaws and eats practically any small animal which it can overpower, as well as dead flesh – captives will readily accept tinned dog food and slices of meat.

Slightly smaller, with a maximum length of around 50 cm (20 in), *A. fuliginosa* (Plate 101) has similar habits. It is rather more slender than the previous species and is attractively marked with irregular black bands and blotches on a white background. It is found in the same general area as *A. alba*, although its range is somewhat larger. The two species co-exist in many places, but it is not known whether they interact.

Many other species of *Amphisbaena* are found throughout South America. Several of these attain relatively large sizes; for instance *A. camura*, which occurs from Bolivia to Argentina, grows to 50 cm (20 in) or more, and several exceed 30 cm (12 in). Most of them are unpigmented, but others, such as *A. angustifrons*, are brown or yellowish in colour. An additional ten species are found in the West Indies, mostly restricted to larger islands such as Cuba, Hispaniola and Puerto Rico, although at least one, *A. fenestrata*, is scattered over a number of small islands. The genus *Cadea* is also found in the West Indies, restricted to

Plate 101. A large South American amphisbaenian, *Amphisbaena fuliginosa.*

Cuba, while *Anops kingi*, the only member of its genus, is found in south-east Brazil and north-east Argentina.

The African amphisbaenids are found mostly south of the Sahara, although one species, *Blanus cinereus*, is found in North Africa and southern Iberia. This small purplish species lives in sandy soil and grows to about 30 cm (12 in). It is rarely seen, although very common in places. It can only be found by turning rocks at certain times of the year – animals which are discovered in this way disappear rapidly down their tunnels if they are not captured immediately. In southern Africa, two amphisbaenids, belonging to the genus *Dalophia*, reach a size of over 50 cm (20 in), but the majority are smaller, 30 cm (12 in) or less. The largest genus, however, is *Monopeltis*, the spade-snouted amphisbaenians, with 16 species in Central and southern Africa. Most are about 30 cm (12 in) in length and are usually unmarked, being pink, although some have lightly pigmented areas on their bodies. The Cape spade-snouted amphisbaenian, *M. capensis*, gives birth to one, two or three live young, but the reproductive method of the others is unknown at present.

TROGONOPHIDAE

The family Trogonophidae has a disjunctive distribution in north-west Africa, Somalia, the Arabian peninsula and Socotra Island in the Indian Ocean. It contains six species, of which five specialise in burrowing through loose sandy soil, and are triangular in cross-section. Several species are attractively marked; for instance, with black spots on a white background. Their breeding habits are unknown. The trogonophid amphisbaenians are unable to autotomise their tails.

RHINEURIDAE

The Rhineuridae contains only one surviving species, *Rhineura floridana.* This species grows to about 25 cm (10 in) and is unpigmented. It is restricted to central and northern Florida, where it lives in areas having dry, sandy soils. It eats small invertebrates such as earthworms and termites and lays eggs. The young are about 10 cm (4 in) long at hatching. They are unable to discard their tails.

BIPEDIDAE

Members of the Bipedidae are ·unique in possessing a front pair of limbs, with which they start their burrow, and which also help them to crawl across the surface. The limbs and digits are large, and situated well forward on the body, so that they look rather like big ears (which is what they are commonly believed to be by local people). There are three

Plate 102. The strange amphisbaenian from Baja California, *Bipes biporus.* (Photograph courtesy of Lee Grismer.)

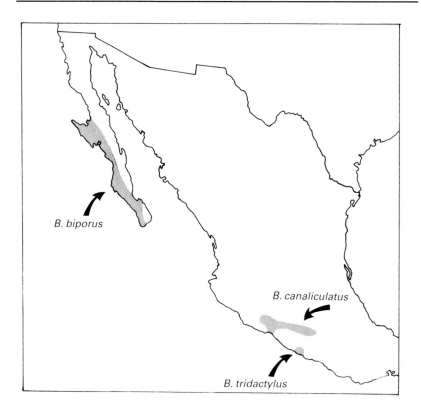

Fig. 17. Distribution of the amphisbaenians genus *Bipes* in Mexico. The distribution patterns of closely related species, especially if they are burrowing forms and therefore not likely to spread by rafting, often hold clues to the movements and origins of landmasses. Here, it seems probable that the southern part of Baja California originally broke away from the west coast of mainland Mexico, taking ancestral *Bipes* stock with it, and drifted north towards Upper California, until it eventually came into contact with the mainland again.

species, all belonging to the genus *Bipes*, all restricted to Mexico, and all capable of discarding their tails. They were the subject of an exhaustive ecological study, published in 1982 (see bibliography), making them the only amphisbaenians which have been thoroughly studied in this way. Among other findings, this research proved that all species of *Bipes* are far more common than were formerly believed – until 1970, less than 50 specimens of all three had been deposited in museums worldwide, whereas by the end of the study a total of over 3,800 had been collected!

The most common and widespread species is the ajolote, *Bipes biporus*, which occurs in the southern half of the Mexican region of Baja California. It lives in dry sandy plains and its tunnel systems often occur around the bases of fence-posts, where termites are also found. In places it is so common that it is frequently found in plant-pots, and may even

185

emerge through the floors of houses if water is spilt, for instance in bathrooms!

The two other species of *Bipes*, *B. canaliculatus* and *B. tridactylus*, are both found on the main Mexican landmass, more precisely in a small dry area on the west coast, bounded by the sea on one side and mountains on the other. These species are less common, and have smaller ranges than *B. biporus*, but are rather similar in appearance. All three species have obviously arisen from the same ancestor, and their present distribution reflects the geological history of this part of the world (Fig. 17). These species are preyed upon by a number of snakes, especially the coral snake, *Micrurus laticollaris*, which has an almost identical range with *B. canaliculatus*, and two other coral snakes in the region.

B. biporus, and presumably the other two species, are voracious predators, ambushing vertebrates and small vertebrates and dragging them into their tunnels to be crushed and torn apart by their powerful jaws. Even sizeable lizards may bear the scars of an unsuccessful attack by a Bipes, in the form of a circle of damaged skin on their bellies. They are usually found within 5 cm (2 in) of the surface, ready to break through if they sense the presence of prey above their tunnel, but may go deeper, up to 20 cm (8 in), during the colder months. They do not hibernate, but are active thoughout the year. The three species lay eggs, ranging in number from one to four, with an average of two. Hatchlings measure about 12 cm (5 in) in length, and emerge at the beginning of summer rains from eggs laid about two months previously, the exact time of year varying among the species due to seasonal differences. It appears that females of two species (*B. biporus* and *B. canaliculatus*) breed only every two or three years, whereas female *B. tridactylus* breed every year. Females of the latter species also mature at least one year earlier than those of the other two.

Bibliography

SECTION 1   LIZARD BIOLOGY AND GENERAL READING

Attenborough, D. (1957), *Zoo Quest for a Dragon*, Lutterworth Press, London.

Bellairs, A. d'A. and Attridge, J. (1975), *Reptiles* (4th edition), Hutchinson University Library, London.

Bogert, C. M. and del Campo, R. M. (1956), 'The Gila monster and its allies: the relationships, habits and behaviour of the lizards of the family Helodermatidae', *Bulletin of the American Museum of Natural History, 109 (1): 1 – 238.*

Brooke, M. de L. and Houston, D. C. (1983), 'The biology and biomass of the skinks *Mabuya sechellensis* and *Mabuya wrightii* on Cousin Island, Seychelles', *Journal of the Zoological Society of London 200: 179 – 195.*

Bustard, H. R. (1970), *Australian Lizards*, Collins, London and Sydney.

Gans, C. (1967), 'A checklist of recent amphisbaenians', *Bulletin of the American Museum of Natural History (135), article 2.*

Gibbons, J. R. H. (1981), 'The biogeography of *Brachylophus* (Iguanidae) including the description of a new species, *B. vitiensis,* from Fiji', *Journal of Herpetology, volume 15, (3): 225 – 273.*

Heatwole, H. (1976), *Reptile Ecology*, University of Queensland Press.

Huey, R. B., Pianka, E. R. and Schoener, T. W. (eds) (1983), *Lizard Ecology*, Harvard University Press, Cambridge, Massachusetts.

Kluge, A. G. (1967), 'Higher taxonomic categories of gekkonid lizards and their evolution', *Bulletin of the American Museum of Natural History, 135: 1 – 59.*

Kluge, A. G. (1974), 'A taxonomic revision of the lizard family Pygopodidae', *Miscellaneous Publications, Museum of Zoology, University of Michigan (152): 1 – 221.*

Kluge, A. G. (1987), 'Cladistic relationships in the Gekkonoidea', *Miscellaneous Publications, Museum of Zoology, University of Michigan (173): iv + 1 – 54*

Lowe, C. H., Schwalbe, C. R. and Johnson, T. B. (1986), *The Venomous Reptiles of Arizona*, Arizona Game and Fish Department.

Mattison, C. (1987), *The Care of Reptiles and Amphibians in Captivity*, (revised edition), Blandford Press, London.

Papenfuss, T. J. (1982), 'The ecology and systematics of the amphisbaenian genus *Bipes*', *Occasional Papers of the California Academy of Sciences, 136: 1 – 42.*

Pearson, O. P. (1954), 'Habits of the lizard *Liolaemus multiformis multiformis* at high altitudes in southern Peru', *Copeia 1954 (2): 111 – 116.*

Pianka, E. R. (1986), *Ecology and Natural History of Desert Lizards*, Princeton University Press, New Jersey.

Sherbrooke, W. C. (1981), *Horned Lizards; Unique Reptiles of Western North America*, Southwest Parks and Monuments Association.

SECTION 2   LIZARD IDENTIFICATION

Arnold, E. N. and Burton, J. A. (1978), *A Field Guide to the Reptiles and Amphibians of Britain and Europe*, Collins, London.

Branch, W. (1988), *Field Guide to the Snakes and other Reptiles of Southern Africa*, Struik, Cape Town and New Holland (Publishers) Ltd., London.

Brown, W. C. and Alcala, A. C. (1978, 1980), *Philippine Lizards* (two volumes), Silliman University, Natural Science, monographs 1 and 2, Dumaguete, Philippines.

Cei, J. M. (1986), *Reptiles del centro, centro-oeste y sur de la Argentina*, Museo Regionale di Scienze Naturali, Turin.

Cogger, H. G. (1983), *Reptiles and Amphibians of Australia* (3rd edition), A. H. & A. W. Reed, Sydney.

Conant, R. (1975), *A Field Guide to Reptiles and Amphibians of Eastern/ Central North America* (2nd edition), Houghton Mifflin Company, Boston.

Duellman, W. E. (1978), 'The biology of an equatorial herpetofauna in Amazonian Ecuador', *Miscellaneous Publications, Museum of Natural History, University of Kansas.*

Frazer, D. (1983), *Reptiles and Amphibians in Britain*, Collins, London.

Hoogmoed, M. S. (1973), *The Lizards and Amphisbaenians of Surinam*, W. Junk, The Hague.

McCoy, M. (1980), *Reptiles of the Solomon Islands*, Wau Ecology Institute, Wau, Papua New Guinea.

Patterson, R. and Bannister, A. (1987), *Reptiles of Southern Africa*, Struik, Cape Town.

Robb, J. (1980), *New Zealand Amphibians and Reptiles*, Collins, Aukland.

Smith, H. M. (1946), *Handbook of Lizards* [of the United States], Cornell University Press, Ithaca, New York.

Smith, M. A. (1935), *The Fauna of British India, Reptilia and Amphibia, Volume II – Sauria,* Taylor and Francis, London.

Stebbins, R. C. (1985), *A Field Guide to Western Reptiles and Amphibians* (2nd edition), Houghton Mifflin Company, Boston.

Storr, G. M., Smith, L. A. and Johnstone, R. E. (1981, 1983), *Lizards of Western Australia*: Part I, Skinks; Part II, Dragons and Monitors, University of Western Australia Press, Perth.

Taylor, E. H. (1963), *The Lizards of Thailand*, University of Kansas Science Bulletin number 64, Lawrence, Kansas.

Vinson, J. and Vinson, J-M. (1969), 'The saurian fauna of the Mascarene Islands', *The Mauritius Institute Bulletin*, Vol. VI, Part 4: 203–320.

JOURNALS

Amphibia–Reptilia (4 per annum), published by the Societas Europaea Herpetologica (The Netherlands).

British Journal of Herpetology (2 per annum) and *British Herpetological Society Bulletin* (4 per annum), published by the British Herpetological Society.

Copeia (4 per annum), published by the American Society of Ichthyologists and Herpetologists.

Herpetofauna (2 per annum), published jointly by the Australian Herpetological Society and the New Zealand Herpetological Society.

Herpetologica (4 per annum), published by the Herpetologists' League (USA).

The Herptile (4 per annum), published by the International Herpetological Society (UK).

Journal of Herpetology (4 per annum) and Herpetological Review (4 per annum), published by the Society for the Study of Reptiles and Amphibians (USA).

Journal of the Herpetological Society of Africa (2 per annum), published by the Herpetological Association of South Africa (South Africa).

The Vivarium (4 per annum), published by the American Federation of Herpetoculturalists.

Index

Numbers in *italic* refer to black and white illustrations.
Numbers in **bold** refer to colour plates.